LETTERS FROM PAUL

An Exegetical Translation

LETTERS FROM PAUL

An Exegetical Translation
by
Boyce W. Blackwelder, M.A., Th.D.

Author of
Light from the Greek New Testament
Toward Understanding Paul
Toward Understanding Romans
Toward Understanding Thessalonians

Warner Press
Anderson, Indiana

227
B568
181643

To
NELLIE
MARGIE
and
MARY ANN

CONTENTS

PREFACE

The Apostle Paul stands as the foremost evangelist and interpreter of the gospel of Christ. More than any other individual, the thinker from Tarsus promoted Christianity's expansion in the Roman Empire, and ultimately the whole Western world came under the influence of his thought.

Paul's Epistles, which form a large part of the New Testament, are letters he wrote to his Christian friends and to various churches. Since man, in his essential nature, never really changes, the personal and social problems of Paul's world are basically the same as those of today. The Apostle dealt with issues in terms of changeless doctrinal and ethical principles. Consequently the truths he enunciated are as relevant for us as they were for believers in the latter part of the first century.

Hellenistic Greek, in which the New Testament is written, was the language generally spoken throughout the Graeco-Roman world. Because of its widespread use and its potential for precise expression, it was especially fitted to serve as the linguistic vehicle for the dissemination of the Christian message.

The term *exegesis*, formed from two Greek words, the preposition *ek, out of,* and the verb *hēgeomai, to lead, guide, unfold, narrate,* refers to the process of getting out of a literary composition the truth contained in it. The aim of biblical exegetics is to make as clear as possible the meaning of the Scriptural text. Thus an interpreter tries to discover what each statement meant to the original writer and to render it accurately into the language at hand.

It is not possible to translate entirely the thought of one language into the thought of another language, but the interpreter works according to the principle of equivalent effect. That is to say, he attempts to translate a document in such a manner that it will produce on his readers the same effect it had on those persons who read it in the first place.

In certain passages the syntax may lend itself to several possible renderings. The translator must make a decision in one direction or another. Working with all the pertinent information at his command, he weighs the salient grammatical and contextual factors and, in the light contributed by all of them, reaches his conclusion.

I have sought to make the present work a translation, not a paraphrase. However, in some instances an interpretive or paraphrastic rendering was necessary in order to express what seemed to be the connotation of the original. I employed brackets to enclose words inserted in an effort to convey meanings implied by particular expressions or contexts. And often, in the interest of clarity, I used explanatory footnotes.

No effort was made to translate the same Greek word in every instance by the same English word. Sometimes because of the contextual coloring, and sometimes for the sake of variety, I translated the same Greek term by different English terms. Actually there are no precise literal English equivalents for many Greek words. Even if there were exact equivalents, they could not be used invariably in every context. Translation is more than a mere word-for-word rendering of one language into another language. Our task is to transfer the idiom characteristic of the Greek into the corresponding idiom characteristic of contemporary English.

I have tried to indicate, at least to some extent, Paul's linguistic versatility and the force of his emotions. (For a detailed treatment of Paul's literary style, see my volume, *Toward Understanding Paul*, Warner Press, 1961, pp. 102-112.) His letters include many long, complex sentences. Should we break these down into shorter units? Perhaps so, at times. However, in order to better acquaint the reader with Paul's literary vigor and masterly command of the language, I retained frequently the long sentence structure. The Apostle's custom of dictating his correspondence to an amanuensis accounts for the fact that his letters follow quite closely the natural flow of oral speech. Although it is interesting and important to reflect a writer's form of expression and manner of style, the prior considerations are accuracy and intelligibility, and I have sought to keep these major goals in mind.

The translation was made from the Greek text edited by Professor Eberhard Nestle, fourth edition, 1904 (London: British and Foreign Bible Society, 1934). The Nestle text is the resultant of a collation of three of the principal recensions of the Greek New Testament prepared in the latter half of the nineteenth century—those of Tischendorf, Westcott and Hort, and Bernhard Weiss. In checking variant readings, I also used Erwin Nestle's *Novum Testamentum Graece* (Stuttgart: Privilegierte Wurttembergische Bibelanstalt, 1932), Augustinus Merk's *Novum Testamentum Graece et Latine* (Rome: Pontifical Biblical Institute, 1944), and the United Bible Societies' *The Greek New Testament* (1966), edited by Kurt Aland, Matthew Black, Bruce M. Metzger, and Allen Wikgren.

No attempt was made to arrange Paul's letters in chronological order, because we cannot speak with certainty about the exact sequence in which they were written. I have followed the arrangement to which we are accustomed in our traditional English versions of the New Testament.

This volume is presented in the hope that its readers may be led into a deeper understanding of the Christian faith as it is delineated by the eminent Apostle.

—Boyce W. Blackwelder

ROMANS

Chapter 1

Paul, a slave of Christ Jesus, a called apostle, in the state of having been set apart for the purpose of [proclaiming] the good news of God, ²which he previously promised through his prophets in writings which by their character are sacred, ³concerning his Son who in relation to humanity became a descendant of David, ⁴but in relation to deity was declared the Son of God with mighty power by the resurrection from the dead—Jesus Christ our Lord; ⁵through whom we received divine favor and apostleship to urge among all nations the obedience which faith produces,ᵃ in behalf of his name, ⁶among whom you also are called ones of Jesus Christ. ⁷To all the beloved of God in Rome, constituted saints in response to [God's] call: May divine favor be yours, and peace, from God our Father and the Lord Jesus Christ.

⁸In the first place, I am giving thanks to my God through Jesus Christ concerning all of you, because the whole world is hearing about [the way in which you are demonstrating] your faith. ⁹For God is my witness, to whom I am rendering spiritual service in [devotion to] the gospel of his Son, how unceasingly I make mention of you, ¹⁰always in my prayers beseeching that somehow now at last I may be permitted by the will of God to come to you. ¹¹For I wish very much to see you, in order that I may impart to you some spiritual benefit, that you may be firmly established. ¹²That is to say, that while I am among you, we may be mutually encouraged by each other's faith, yours being a blessing to me and mine to you.

¹³I want you to know too, [my] brothers, that many times I planned to come to you (but responsibilities elsewhereᵇ prevented me), in order that I might gather some fruit among you as well as among other Gentiles.ᶜ ¹⁴Both to Greeks and to barbarians, both to

---

ᵃRendering *pisteōs, faith,* as subjective genitive.
ᵇCf. 15:20-22.   ᶜOr, among the rest of the nations.

13

the educated and to the uneducated, I am held by an obligation. [15]So, as far as my own willingness is concerned,[d] I am eager to preach the gospel to you in Rome also. [16]For I am not ashamed of the gospel: indeed, by its very nature it is God's own power by which he saves every person who is trusting [in the message], both Jew and Greek alike.[e] [17]For in it is revealed God's kind of righteousness —[the righteousness] which is entirely by faith,[f] just as it stands written, "Now the man who is righteous on the basis of faith shall live."[g]

[18]Certainly the holy wrath of God is constantly being revealed from heaven against all the impiety and unrighteousness of men who in wickedness are suppressing the truth, [19]because that which is known about God is manifest within them: indeed God made it evident to them. [20]For the invisible things of him—both his eternal power and divine nature—ever since the creation of the world have been clearly discernible by means of the things [he] made, so that they are utterly without excuse.

[21]Although having been acquainted with God, they did not glorify him as God, nor did they show gratitude, but they became futile in their reasonings and their foolish hearts were darkened. [22]Pretending to be wise, they became stupid, [23]and they exchanged the glory of the incorruptible God for a likeness of an image of perishable man, and of winged creatures, four-footed beasts, and reptiles. [24]So then, because of the sinful cravings of their hearts, God gave them over to uncleanness which resulted in the degrading of their bodies among themselves. [25]They exchanged the truth of God for falsehood, and worshiped and served the creature rather than the Creator who is blessed forever. Amen.

[26]For this reason God abandoned them to passions of dishonor. Actually even their women[h] changed the natural function of sex into that which is contrary to nature. [27]Indeed, in like manner also, the males, having disregarded the natural function of the females, were inflamed with lust for each other; males engaging in shameful prac-

---

[d]Literally, *as the* [situation] *according to me* [is].

[e]Or, the Jew first, but also the Greek.

[f]Literally, *out of faith into faith.* Paul emphasizes the fact that righteousness begins and continues in faith.   [g]Hab. 2:4.

[h]Greek, *thēleiai, females.* Paul's use of the terms *females* and *males,* instead of *women* and *men* in his reference to homosexual vices in verses 26-27, denotes the low level of the immoral practices which he condemns.

tices with males, and duly receiving in their own persons the retribution which was the inescapable penalty of such error.

28And inasmuch as they decided not to give proper acknowledgment to God, he gave them over to a mind insensible to reproof, to detestable practices. 29They reached a state in which they were filled with all unrighteousness, wickedness, covetousness, degeneracy; full of envy, murder, strife, deceit, evil disposition. 30They were secret slanderers, evil speakers, hateful to God.[i] They delighted in hurting others. They were haughty, boastful, inventors of evil devices, disobedient to parents, 31void of [spiritual and moral] discernment, untrustworthy, without affection for those who should have been dear to them because of the ties of kinship, having no pity. 32Although having known well the inexorable mandate of God, that those who engage in such things deserve death, they not only do them, but heartily approve others [j] who practice them.

Chapter 2

Therefore you are without excuse, O man, whoever you are, who assumes the role of a critic. For the very fact that you are judging the other person brings condemnation upon yourself because you, the critic, are practicing the things you condemn.[a] 2Now we know that God's verdict is in accordance with truth against those who practice such things. 3And you, O man, who criticizes those who are committing such things, yet all the while doing them [yourself], do you suppose that you will escape the condemnation of God? 4Or do you spurn the wealth of his kindness and toleration and longsuffering, unaware of the fact that such gracious treatment is God's effort to lead you to a change of mind?[b]

5But according to your obstinacy and impenitent heart, you are heaping up retribution against yourself for the day of the wrath and the manifestation of the righteous judgment of God, 6who will give every man what is due him according to his deeds: 7eternal life to those who with endurance in good work are seeking glory and honor and immortality; 8but wrath and indignation to those who out

---

iOr, haters of God. jLiterally, *the ones.*
aLiterally, *the same things.* bOr, to repentance.

of self-interest employ subtle schemes of evasion, and do not obey the truth but are obedient to unrighteousness. [9]Extreme distress and inescapable calamity [will come] upon every human soul who persists in practicing evil, upon both Jew and Greek alike.[c] [10]But [there will be] glory and honor and peace for every person who is performing the good, for Jew and Greek alike.[d] [11]Certainly there is no partiality with God!

[12]Now as many as sinned without law will also perish without law. And as many as sinned in the sphere of law will be judged by law. [13]For it is not the hearers of law who are righteous before God, but the doers of law will be declared righteous. [14]Actually, when the Gentiles, who have no law, intuitively do the things required by the law, they, having no law, are a law to themselves. [15]They demonstrate the effect of the law written in their hearts, their conscience bearing witness with them, and their moral reflections accusing or else defending them, [16]in the day when, according to my gospel, God through Christ Jesus exercises judgment upon the secret things of men.

[17]Now you who take the name of Jew for yourself, and rely upon law, and boast of God's favor, [18]and know his will, and are able to discriminate between moral values,[e] being habitually instructed out of the Law; [19]having convinced yourself that you are indeed a guide to the blind, a light to the ones in darkness, [20]a corrector of the stupid, a teacher of infants, because you have in the Law the representation of knowledge and of the truth—[21]you, therefore, who are teaching others, you teach yourself, do you not?

You who declare that one should not steal, do you steal? [22]You who prohibit adultery, do you commit adultery? You who voice such horror about contamination with idols, do you deal in idolatrous objects for gain?[f] [23]You who are making a boast regarding law, do you by transgression of the Law dishonor God? [24]Indeed, just as it stands written, "The name of God is blasphemed among the Gentiles because of you."[g]

[25]Now anything of the character of circumcision indeed is profitable if you practice the Law. But if you are a transgressor of the

---

cOr, upon the Jew first, but also upon the Greek.
dOr, for the Jew first, but also for the Greek.
eOr, between things that differ.　　　　　　fLiterally, *do you plunder shrines?*
gIsa. 52:5, adaptation from the Septuagint.

Law, your circumcision has reached a state in which it is the equivalent of uncircumcision. 26If, on the other hand, the uncircumcised man keeps the moral requirements of the Law, his uncircumcision will be accounted as the equivalent of circumcision, will it not? 27The man who is physically uncircumcised and yet fulfills the Law will condemn you who have the letter [of the Law] and are physically circumcised, and yet transgress the Law. 28In fact, he who has the outward marks is not a Jew; neither is true circumcision a physical thing; 29but the real Jew is one inwardly, and real circumcision is of the heart, in the spirit, not in the letter. The praise of such an individual comes not from men but from God.

Chapter 3

Then what advantage does the Jew have? Or of what benefit is circumcision? 2Much in every way. First, because the Jews were entrusted with God's message. 3What if some of them did prove unfaithful? Their unfaithfulness does not nullify God's faithfulness, does it? 4By no means! But even if every man is a liar, let God always be true, as it stands written, "That thou mayest be vindicated in thy words, and win the verdict any time thou art judged."[a]

5But if our unrighteousness exhibits the righteousness of God, what shall we say? God is not unjust when he inflicts retribution, is he? (I speak according to a human way of thinking.[b]) 6Not at all! If that were true, how could God judge the world? 7Furthermore, if the truth of God abounded to his glory because of my falsehood, why am I still being judged as a sinner? 8And why not say—as we are reproachfully charged, and as some allege that we assert—Let us do evil that good may come? The condemnation of those [who make such an allegation] is just.

9What about it then? Have we advantage for ourselves? Not in every way; for we have already brought charge against both Jews and Greeks, that they are all under sin. 10Thus it stands written:

There is not a righteous person, not even one!
11No one understands, no one is seeking after God.

---

[a]Ps. 51:4.   [b]Or, I use an argument such as men would employ.

¹²All have deviated from the right way. All to a man have become corrupt. No one habitually does good, not so much as one!

¹³Their throat is a grave standing open. With their tongues they have talked deceitfully. The poison of deadly serpents is under their lips.

¹⁴Their mouth is full of cursing and bitterness.

¹⁵Their feet are swift to shed blood.

¹⁶Devastation and misery are in their wake,

¹⁷And the way of peace they have not known.

¹⁸There is no reverence of God before their eyes.[c]

¹⁹Now we know that whatever the Law says, it speaks to those who are within the jurisdiction of the Law, in order that every mouth may be silenced and all the world become liable to God's judgment; ²⁰because no individual will be pronounced righteous before him on the ground of obedience to law. Actually, all law can do is bring a full awareness of sin.

²¹But now God's kind of righteousness stands manifested apart from law [of any kind], although it is attested by the Law and the Prophets. ²²Indeed God's kind of righteousness is through faith in Jesus Christ. It is effective for all who are trusting [in him]. ²³There is no distinction, for the whole race has sinned, and [man] continues to fall short of God's standard. ²⁴The permanent principle of justification operates freely by the gift of his grace through the redemption which is in Christ Jesus, ²⁵whom God openly set forth as the means of expiation by his blood, to be appropriated through faith. This was to demonstrate God's righteousness, inasmuch as in his forbearance he had tolerated the previously committed sins. ²⁶He did so, with a view to the display of his righteousness in the present time, that he might be righteous himself even while declaring righteous the person who places trust in Jesus.

²⁷Then what becomes of human boasting? It is shut out completely! On what sort of principle? On that of works? No, but on the principle of faith. ²⁸For we conclude that a man is declared righteous by faith, apart from any works of law. ²⁹Or [is God] the God of the Jews only? [He is the God] of the Gentiles also, is he not? Yes, also of the Gentiles, ³⁰since it is a fact that there is but one God. He will declare

---

cCompounded quotation. Cf. Pss. 5:9; 10:7; 14:1-3; 36:1; 140:3; Isa. 59:7-8.

righteous the circumcision on the basis of faith, and the uncircumcision by means of faith. [31]Does this mean that we nullify law through[d] this faith? Not at all! Instead, we establish law in its proper place.

Chapter 4

What are we to infer about the status[a] of Abraham our natural forefather? [2]Now if Abraham was declared righteous on the basis of works, he has ground for boasting—but not before God. [3]For what does the Scripture say? "And Abraham believed[b] God, and his faith was counted to him for righteousness."[c]

[4]Now to the individual who works, the pay is not considered as a favor but as an obligation. [5]But the person who does not rely upon work, but is depending upon him who declares righteous the ungodly, that person's faith is counted for righteousness. [6]Even so, David declares the spiritual well-being of the man to whom God counts righteousness apart from works: [7]"Supremely happy are they whose lawless acts have been forgiven, whose sins have been covered over! [8]Supremely happy is the person whose sin the Lord will not at all count against him!"[d]

[9]Now is this spiritual well-being for the circumcised only, or for the uncircumcised also? We reiterate, Abraham's faith was counted to him for righteousness. [10]Actually in what circumstances was it thus counted? Was it after he was circumcised, or before he was circumcised? It was not after he was circumcised, but before. [11]And he received a sign consisting of circumcision which was a seal to certify the righteousness which was his by faith which he had before he was circumcised, that he might be the father of all who believe, even though they are uncircumcised, that this righteousness might be counted to them; [12]and that he might be the father of those who are not merely circumcised but who also walk in the steps of our father Abraham in the faith which he had prior to circumcision.

[13]For the promise to Abraham or to his posterity that he should be the heir of the world did not come through anything in the cate-

---

[d]Or, by means of.
[a]Force of perfect infinitive of *heuriskō, to find.*
[b]*Episteuse, he believed,* is placed first in the Greek clause for emphasis.
[c]Gen. 15:6.   [d]Ps. 32:1-2.

gory of law, but through the righteousness conditioned on faith.
14For if those who depend on law be heirs, faith stands emptied of
significance and the promise is permanently nullified. 15Indeed,
the law continually produces wrath; but where there is no law, neither
is there transgression.

16This is why fulfillment hinges on faith, in order that it might be
a matter of unmerited favor, so that the promise might be assured for
all the progeny, not only for those [whose background is] of the
Law, but also for those who have the kind of faith exercised by
Abraham, (who is the father of us all, 17just as it stands written, "I
have constituted you the father of many nations,"e) before him whom
he believed, [even before] God who reanimates the dead and who
summons nonexistent things as if they already existed.

18In a situation which was hopeless, [Abraham] had hope: he
believed that he would become the father of many nations according
to the declaration, "Thus shall your descendants be."f 19He never
even weakened in faith when he considered the impotent state of
his own body—he was about a hundred years old—and Sarah's in-
capacity for motherhood. 20Indeed, because of the promise of God,
he did not waver between certainty and uncertainty, but was empowered by faith. He gave glory—and praise—to God, 21and was fully
convinced that what God had promised he was able also to accomplish. 22For this reason [Abraham's faith] was counted to him for
righteousness.

23Now it was not because of him only that the statement, "It was
counted to him," was written. 24But it was also for our benefit, to
whom it is about to be counted, trusting [as we areg] in him who
raised from the dead Jesus our Lord, 25who was delivered up because
of our misdeeds, and who was raised to life for our justification.

Chapter 5

Therefore having been justified on the basis of faith, let us keep
on enjoying peace with God through our Lord Jesus Christ, 2by whom
also we have obtained the introductiona by faith into this state of

---

eGen. 17:5.   fGen. 15:5.
gLiterally, *the ones who are trusting.*   aOr, access.

divine favor in which we remain standing. And let us continue jubilant because of our hope of [sharing in] God's glory. 3And not only [do we contemplate future joys], but even in the midst of the [usual] hardships let us go on being jubilant. For we are aware that hardship develops perseverance, 4perseverance [develops] proved character, and proved character [develops] expectation. 5And this expectation never disappoints, because God's love has been poured forth into and continues inundating our hearts through the Holy Spirit who has been given to us.

6Indeed, while we were still weak, Christ at the proper time died in behalf of the ungodly. 7Why, very rarely in behalf of a righteous man will anyone give his life, although in behalf of such*b* a good man perhaps someone might even dare to die. 8But God gives proof of his own love for us by the fact that while we were yet sinners, Christ died in our behalf. 9Therefore, since we have now been declared righteous by means of his blood, much more shall we be saved through him from the wrath [to come]. 10For if while being enemies we were reconciled to God through the death of his Son, much more, now that we have been reconciled, we shall be saved by his life. 11And not only so, but we are jubilant continually in God through our Lord Jesus Christ, through whom we have now received this reconciliation.

12[Look at the situation in this perspective:] Just as through one man sin entered into the world, and through sin came death, even so death passed through to all men, because all sinned. 13Certainly sin was in the world prior to the Law, but sin is not charged against a person where there is no law [of any kind]. 14Nevertheless, death reigned from Adam until Moses even over those who did not violate an explicitly revealed command, as did Adam, who is a figure of the One who was to come.

15But there is a contrast between the misdeed and the gracious gift. For if by the misdeed of that one man the many died, much more did the favor of God and the gift bestowed by grace through the one man, Jesus Christ, abound for the many. 16Also there is a contrast between the effects of that one man's sin and the effects of the gift. For the sentence occasioned by one man's misdeed was a verdict of condemnation, whereas the gracious gift occasioned by

*b*Literally, *the good man.*

the misdeeds of many results in a verdict of acquittal. [17]For if by the misdeed of the one man death reigned through that one, much more will those who are receiving the abundance of God's[c] favor and his[d] gift of righteousness reign in life through the One, Jesus Christ.

[18]Accordingly then, as through one misdeed condemnation came upon all men,[e] even so through one righteous act there comes to all men life-giving acquittal.[f] [19]For even as by the disobedience of the one man the many were constituted sinners, even so by the obedience of the One the many will be constituted righteous. [20]Law, in addition, came in alongside to accentuate the gravity and enormous scope of the misdeed. But however prevalent and powerful the sum total of sin may be, God's grace has abounded more exceedingly, [21] so that just as sin reigned by death, even so grace might reign by means of righteousness resulting in life eternal through Jesus Christ our Lord.

Chapter 6

What inference then are we to draw? May we remain on in sin in order that God's grace may multiply? [2]Away with the thought! How can we, the very persons who died to sin, live in it any longer? [3]Or do you not realize that as many of us as were baptized [as a public declaration of dedication[a]] to Christ Jesus were baptized to picture his death? [4]Therefore we are buried together with him through this baptism which pictures his death, so that just as Christ was raised up from the dead by the glory of the Father, thus we too might demonstrate a new quality of life. [5]For if we have become united with him in the likeness of his death, indeed also we shall be [united with him in the likeness] of his resurrection. [6]This we know, that our former self was crucified with him, in order that the body as the instrument of sin might be rendered inoperative, so that we should no longer go on being slaves of sin. [7]Indeed, the person who has [thus] died stands acquitted of sin.

[8]Now in view of the fact that we died with Christ, we believe that we shall also live with him, [9]realizing that Christ, having been

---

cLiterally, *the favor.*   dLiterally, *the gift.*

eOr, condemnation resulted for all men.

fOr, life-giving acquittal resulted for all men.

aImplied by preposition and context. In the papyri, *eis* is used with *onoma, name,* to denote possession.

raised up from the dead, will never die again. Death no longer has any dominion over him. [10]For in his death, he died to sin once [in one consummate, never-to-be-repeated act[b]]. But the life he lives, he is living to God. [11]Thus also you must consider[c] yourselves as dead indeed to sin, but alive to God in Christ Jesus.

[12]Therefore you must not let sin reign in your mortal bodies, causing you to obey their evil desires; [13]neither be presenting your bodily faculties as instruments of unrighteousness in the [service of] sin. But present yourselves now and completely to God as individuals brought from death to life,[d] and [present] your bodily faculties as instruments of righteousness to God. [14]For nothing of the character of sin shall have dominion over you, for you are not under law but under [God's] favor.

[15]In the light of this fact, what is to be our course of action? Shall we commit sin occasionally, because we are not under law but under grace? Certainly not! [16]Do you not realize that to whom you yield yourselves as slaves for obedience, you are slaves of him whom you obey, whether of sin which results in death, or of obedience which results in righteousness? [17]But thanks be to God! Although you once were slaves of sin, you became obedient from your hearts to the standard of doctrine unto which you were delivered, [18]and, having been liberated from sin, you were enslaved to righteousness.

[19](I use an analogy from human relations, on account of the weakness of your natural apprehension.) For just as you [previously] surrendered your bodily faculties to the bondage of uncleanness and to more and more lawlessness, so now completely surrender your bodily faculties to the slavery of righteousness for the development of holiness. [20]For when you were slaves of sin, righteousness exerted no control over you. [21]What was the result of such behavior? Things of which you are now ashamed! For the consummation of those things is death. [22]But now, having been set free from sin, and enslaved to God, you are bearing the fruit of progress in holiness, and the ultimate destiny is eternal life.

[23]Mark it well: Sin pays wages in kind, which is death, but the gracious gift of God is life eternal in Christ Jesus our Lord.

---

[b]Denoted by aorist tense and adverb *ephapax, only once.*
[c]Rendering *logizesthe* as imperative, not indicative.
[d]Or, as alive from the dead.

Chapter 7

Surely you know, [my] brothers—for I am speaking to persons who understand the nature of law—that the law has jurisdiction over an individual only during the extent of his lifetime! [2]For example, a married woman remains bound by law to her husband while he is living. But if her husband dies, she stands completely released from the law regarding the husband. [3]Consequently, if she marries another man while her husband is living, she will be designated an adulteress. But if her husband dies, she is free from his legal claim, so that she is not an adulteress if she marries another man.

[4]Just so, my brothers, you also were rendered dead to the Law through the body of Christ, so that you might belong to another—to him who was raised up from the dead—in order that we might bring forth fruit for God. [5]For when we were motivated by natural impulses, sin's inclinations, irritated by legal restraint, were operative in our bodily faculties, producing a harvest for death. [6]But now we have been completely released from the Law, having died [to that] in which we were being held fast, so that we are rendering service in newness of spirit[a] and not in oldness of letter.[b]

[7]What is the implication of this? Is the Law [itself] bad? Certainly not! However I would not have realized what sin meant had it not been for law. For instance, I would not have been aware of covetousness if the Law had not said, "You must not desire what is forbidden."[c] [8]Indeed, sin, having obtained a base of operation by means of the commandment, aroused in me every kind of illicit desire—for apart from law, sin lay dormant.

[9]Actually at one time I was alive without awareness of the Law. But when the commandment came, sin was stirred into activity, and I died. [10]And so, for me, this very commandment which was intended for life resulted in death. [11]For sin, having received a base of operation by means of the commandment, completely beguiled me and used it to slay me. [12]So the Law [itself is] holy, and the commandment [is] holy and just and good.

[13]Does this mean that something which is good became death for me? Not at all! But sin, that it might be exposed as sin, worked out

---

aOr, newness of the Spirit.   bOr, oldness of legal code.
cExod. 20:17; Deut. 5:21.

death to me through that which is good. Thus, by means of the commandment, the utterly horrible nature of sin becomes evident. [14]For we know that the Law is spiritual, but I am[d] constituted of weak human nature, in the state of having been sold under sin's power. [15]Actually I am perplexed by my own behavior: for I am not doing what I want to do, but I am practicing what I hate. [16]But if I practice what I do not want to do, I acknowledge that the Law is excellent.

[17]In fact, it is not I myself committing such things, but [it is] the sin within me. [18]For I know that in me, that is, in my unregenerate nature, nothing good dwells. The will to do right is constantly with me, but the performance of it is not. [19]Indeed, I am not doing the good that I want to do, but I am practicing the evil that I do not want to do. [20]But if I am practicing what I do not want to do, it is really not I myself doing it, but the sin which is dwelling in me. [21]Accordingly I find this antimony:[e] although I want to practice the good, the evil is constantly present with me. [22]Certainly in my inmost self I endorse God's law, [23]but I find another principle of a different kind operating in my bodily faculties, warring against the force of my reason, and bringing me into captivity to the power of the sin which is expressive in my bodily faculties. [24]What a miserable man I am! Who will deliver me from this death which enslaves the body?[f] [25]Thanks be to God [who gives deliverance] through Jesus Christ our Lord! Accordingly then,[g] I myself with my better judgment serve the law of God, but with the old nature the principle of sin.

Chapter 8

Consequently there is now no condemnation whatsoever for those who are in Christ Jesus. [2]For the principle[a] of the Spirit of life in Christ Jesus has liberated you[b] from the principal[a] of sin and death. [3]Indeed, what was impossible for the Law—because it continued weak, being limited by human nature which was the medium in which it had to function—[God accomplished], having sent his own

---

[d]In vv. 14–25, Paul uses the present tense, probably for vividness.
[e]Rendering *nomos* in this context of opposing laws, i.e. forces of action.
[f]Literally, *from the body of this death.*
[g]V.25b seems to be a summary statement of the conflict described in the preceding verses.   [a]Or, force of action.
[b]Second person singular. Some manuscripts have *me*.

Son in the likeness[c] of sinful nature, and concerning sin, overcame[d] sin in human nature, [4]in order that the righteous requirement of the Law might be fully met in us who do not live by the impulses of the old nature, but by [the motivation of] the Spirit.

[5]For individuals who are living according to the old nature have sensual inclinations, but those [who are] living according to the Spirit have spiritual inclinations. [6]The attitude prompted by the old nature [means] death, but the attitude prompted by the Spirit [means] life and peace. [7]Now the attitude prompted by the old nature is hostility toward God. For it does not subject itself to the Law of God—indeed it cannot. [8]Hence it is impossible for people who are dominated by the old nature to please God.

[9]But you are not dominated by the old nature but by the Spirit, if it is a fact that the Spirit of God is dwelling in you. And if any person does not have the Spirit of Christ, such a person[e] is not of him. [10]But if Christ is in you, then although death is inevitable for the body[f] because of sin, yet the spirit[g] [is] life because of righteousness. [11]And if the Spirit of him who raised Jesus from the dead is dwelling in you, he who raised Christ Jesus from the dead will also reanimate your mortal bodies through[h] his Spirit who is dwelling in you.

[12]So then, [my] brothers, we are not obligated to the old nature, to live under its control. [13]For if you live under the control of the old nature, you are heading straight for impending doom.[i] But if by the Spirit you keep putting to death the [improper] deeds of the body, you will continue to live.

[14]For as many as are being led by the Spirit of God, these are the sons of God. [15]Indeed, you did not receive a spirit of bondage, [to place you] again into [an attitude of] dread. But you received the spirit[j] of sonship in which [k] we exclaim, "O God, our Father!" [16]The Spirit himself witnesses together with the witness of our spirit that we are children of God. [17]And if children, also heirs—God's heirs and Christ's coheirs—if we really share his sufferings, so that we may also share his glory.

---

[c]Paul is saying that Christ came to share our nature, apart from its sinfulness.
[d]Or, condemned.
[e]Literally, *this one*.   [f]Literally, *the body* [is] *dead.*
[g]Or, Spirit.   [h]Some manuscripts read, "because of his Spirit," etc.
[i]Literally, *you are about to die.*
[j]Or, the Spirit.   [k]Or, by whom.

18Actually, I regard the sufferings of this present period unworthy of consideration in view of the glory about to be unveiled with reference to us. 19Indeed, the creation, with intense longing, is waiting eagerly for the sons of God to be revealed. 20For the creation was subjected to frustration, not by its own choice, but on account of him who subjected [it]. 21[But this was done] in hope, because even the creation itself will be liberated from the bondage of decay [and will be brought] into the glorious freedom of the children of God. 22For we know that the whole creation continues groaning together and sharing birth pangs until now.

23And not only that, but even we ourselves, who have the Spirit as the foretaste*l* [of the future glory], are inwardly groaning while awaiting attentively [the culmination of] sonship, the redemption of our bodies. 24Indeed in this hope we were saved. A hope seen is not hope, for who hopes for what he sees? 25But if we hope for what we do not see, we wait eagerly for it with endurance.

26Likewise also the Spirit gives assistance in our weakness—he takes hold [of our problems] on the other side*m* —for we do not know what we should pray for as we ought, but the Spirit himself intercedes in our behalf in the groanings which are unutterable. 27And the Searcher of hearts knows the intercessory purpose of the Spirit, that according to [the will of] God he pleads in behalf of [his] consecrated ones.*n* 28And we know that for those who continue loving God, for those who are the called ones*o* according to [his] purpose, God works all things together for good. 29Those whom he foreapproved, he also planned in advance to be conformed to the image of his Son, that he might be the Ideal Representative*p* [as the first to rise from the dead] among many brothers. 30And those whom he planned in advance, he also called. And those whom he called, he also declared righteous. And those whom he declared righteous, he also glorified.

31What therefore are we to conclude in view of these things? If God is for us, who [can be] against us? 32Will not he who went so

---

*l*Literally, *firstfruits.* In the papyri *aparchē* has such meanings as *entrance fee* and *birth certificate.*

*m*Rendering *sunantilambanetai,* present indicative of double compound verb which means *to take hold at the opposite end together with.*

*n*Or, saints.

*o*The *called* refers to those who have heard God's invitation and have responded affirmatively. For other examples of this Pauline concept, cf. 8:30; 9:24; 1 Cor. 1:2, 24.

*p*Literally, *the Firstborn.*

far as not to spare his own Son, but delivered him up in behalf of us all, also with him freely give us all things [in the whole sphere of salvation]?*q* 33Who can bring any charge against God's chosen ones? God is the one who declares righteous! 34Who can condemn [us]? Is it Christ Jesus who died, and beyond that was raised up, who is at the right hand of God, and who is actually interceding in our behalf?

35What can separate us from the love which Christ has for us? Can hardship, or distress, or persecution, or famine, or nakedness, or peril, or sword? 36As it stands written: 36"For thy sake we are being put to death all day long; we were regarded as sheep doomed to slaughter."*r* 37But in all these things we are winning an overwhelming victory through him who loved us. 38For I stand fully convinced that neither death, nor life, nor angels, nor rulers, nor things present, nor things to come, nor powers, 39nor any dimension of space,*s* nor anything in all creation will be able to separate us from the love of God which is in Christ Jesus our Lord!

Chapter 9

I am speaking the truth in Christ—I do not falsify, [for] my conscience, directed by the Holy Spirit, bears me witness—2that I have great grief and unceasing sorrow in my heart. 3Actually I was on the point of wishing even myself accursed from the Christ in place of*a* my brethren, my natural kinsmen, 4they who are Israelites, to whom belonged the privileges of sonship, and the [Shekinah] glory, and the covenants, and the giving of the Law, and the temple service, and the promises, 5and the patriarchs, and from whom—from the standpoint of human descent—came the Christ who is over all, God blessed forever. Amen.

6But this is not implying that the word of God has reached a state of ineffectiveness. Indeed, not all those who descended from Israel constitute [the true] Israel, 7nor are they all Abraham's children [in the sense of heirs] because they descended from him. But [the promise was], "In Isaac shall offspring be named for thee."*b*

8That is to say, those who are natural descendants are not [thereby] the children of God, but those designated children by the promise are

---

qLiterally, *the all things.*   rPs. **44**:22.
sLiterally, *nor height nor depth.*   aOr, in behalf of.   bGen. 21.12.

considered [Abraham's] offspring. [9]For this statement is a promise: "I will intervene, and about this time next year Sarah shall have a son."[c] [10]Furthermore, there is also [the incident of] Rebecca who was with child by Isaac our forefather. [11][Although the same man[d] was the father of both children,] before the twin sons[e] were born or had done anything good or bad, in order that God's purpose of choice might remain—[12]which depends not on human works but on the One calling—it was said to her, "The greater shall serve the lesser."[f] [13]Thus it stands written: "Jacob I loved, but Esau I hated."[g]

[14]What then are we to infer? There is no injustice with God, is there? Absolutely not! [15]Indeed, he says to Moses, "I will have mercy on whom I choose to have mercy. And I will have compassion on whom I choose to have compassion."[h] [16]Accordingly, therefore, mercy is not [a matter] of man's[i] resolve or effort, but of God who extends it.

[17]For the Scripture says of Pharaoh, "I have raised you up for the express purpose of displaying my power in you. And to proclaim my name in all the earth."[j] [18]Thus [God] has mercy on whom he will, and he hardens whom he will.

[19]Then you will ask me, Why does he still go on blaming [men for their deeds]? Actually who can maintain resistance against his resolve? [20]But the question really is: Who are you, a mere man, to engage in controversy with God? Does the thing formed say to the one having formed it, Why did you make me like this? [21]Has not the potter authority over the clay to make out of the same mass one vessel for a lofty use and another for a lowly use? [22]Then what if God, although willing to manifest his wrath and to make known his power, tolerated with much long-suffering the objects of indignation even though they were in a state of readiness for destruction, [23]and [did so] in order to make known the riches of his glory upon the objects of mercy, which he previously prepared for glory, [24]even us whom he has called, not only from among the Jews but also from among the Gentiles?

---

[c]Gen. 18:10, 14.   [d]Indicated by *ex henos, of one* [husband], v. 10.

[e]Indicated by masculine plural participles, *gennēthentōn, were born,* and *praxantōn, had done,* in light of original account of twins in Gen. 25:22-24.   [f]Gen. 25:23.

[g]Mal. 1:2-3. There is no animosity with God. "I hated" is an anthropopathic expression which refers to the result of divine selection. God may be said to "love less" only by comparison in the sense that Esau was not made the third patriarch.

[h]Exod. 33:19.   [i]Or, one's.   [j]Exod. 9:16.

25As, in fact, he says in Hosea, "A people which were not mine, I will call my people; and she who was not beloved, [I will call] beloved. 26And in the place where it was said to them, 'You are not my people,' there they shall be called sons of the living God."[k]

27Moreover Isaiah exclaims concerning Israel, "Although the number of the sons of Israel be as the sand of the sea, only the remnant will be saved. 28For completely and speedily will the Lord accomplish his word upon the earth."[l] 29Also as Isaiah previously said, "If the Lord of hosts had not left us survivors, we would have become like Sodom, and would have resembled Gomorrah."[m]

30What conclusion do we reach? That Gentiles, who were not pursuing righteousness, have grasped it,[n] even the righteousness conditioned on faith; 31whereas Israel, pursuing a law characterized by righteousness, did not attain to [such] a law. 32Why? Because [they sought it] by works rather than by faith. They tripped over the stumbling-stone, 33just as it stands written: "Behold I place in Zion a stone on which men stumble and a mighty Rock of impediment; but the one who trusts in him will not be put to shame."[o]

Chapter 10

Brethren, that which would give my heart the greatest satisfaction, and that for which I pray to God on behalf [of my kinsmen], is [their] salvation. 2Of course I can testify that they have zeal for God, but it is [zeal] not based upon sufficient knowledge. 3For, disregarding the righteousness that comes from God, and seeking to establish their own, they did not yield themselves to the righteousness of God. 4Indeed, Christ is the fulfillment [of everything in the whole realm] of law for righteousness to every individual who is trusting [in him].

5Moses writes[a] that the man who can perform the righteousness required by law will live by [that righteousness]. 6But the righteousness which faith produces speaks thus: Do not say in your heart, Who will ascend into heaven (that is, to bring Christ down)? 7or, Who will descend into the abyss (that is, to bring Christ up from the dead)? 8But what does it say? The utterance is near you, on your lips, even

---

[k]Hos. 1:10; 2:23   [l]Isa. 10:22-23; 28:22.   [m]Isa. 1:9.
[n]Literally, *righteousness*.   [o]Isa. 8:14; 28:16.   [a]Lev. 18:5.

in your heart[b] (that is, the utterance about faith which we are proclaiming): [9]If you acknowledge with your mouth that Jesus is Lord, and believe in your heart that God raised him from the dead, you will be saved.

[10]For with the heart a person exercises faith that brings righteousness, and with the mouth he makes the acknowledgment that brings salvation. [11]For the Scripture says, "No one who trusts in him will be put to shame."[c] [12]Indeed there is no distinction between Jew and Greek, for the same universal Lord is abounding in resources [accessible] to all who call upon him. [13] For absolutely everyone who calls upon the name of the Lord will be saved.[d]

[14]But how can men call upon him in whom they have not believed? And how can they believe in him of whom they have not heard? And how can they hear unless someone preaches? [15]And how can they preach unless they are sent with a commission? As it stands written, "How welcome is the coming[e] of those who announce the glad tidings of good things!"[f]

[16]But not all obeyed the glad news. Indeed, Isaiah asks, "Lord, who has believed our message?"[g] [17]So then, faith [comes] from what is heard, and what is heard [comes] through the utterance about Christ. [18]But I ask, It was not that they never heard, was it? Of course they heard! "Their voice went forth into all the earth, and their words into the extremities of the inhabitable world."[h]

[19]Again I ask, Israel did not fail to know, did they? First, Moses says, "I myself will make you jealous by those who are no nation. By a people without understanding, I will anger you."[i]

[20]Moreover, Isaiah is daring enough to say, "I was found by those not seeking me. I became manifest to those not inquiring for me."[j] [21]But of Israel he says, "All day long I stretched forth my hands to a disobedient and obstinate people."[k]

Chapter 11

I ask, therefore, God did not thrust away from himself his people, did he? Certainly not! In fact, I myself am an Israelite, a descendant

---

[b]Deut. 30:11-14. [e]Isa. 28:16. [d]Joel 2:32.
[c]Literally, *how beautiful are the feet.* [f]Isa. 52:7. [g]Isa. 53:1.
[h]Ps. 19:4. [i]Deut. 32:21. [j]Isa. 65:1. [k]Isa. 65:2.

of Abraham, of the tribe of Benjamin. 2God did not thrust away from himself his people whom he foreapproved. Surely you know what the Scripture says in the passage about Elijah, how he pleads with God against Israel: 3"Lord, they have killed thy prophets and destroyed thy altars. I am the only one left, and they seek my life."*a*

4But what was the divine answer to him? "I have kept back for myself seven thousand men who have never bowed a knee to Baal."*b* 5Likewise, even in the present period there has come to be a remnant, selected on the principle of [God's] gracious favor. 6But if it is by [his] gracious favor, it certainly is not on the basis of works. Otherwise favor loses its character as favor.

7Then what are we to infer? Israel has never obtained that which it is still seeking, but the chosen ones have obtained it. 8The rest have been hardened, just as it stands written: "God gave them over to an attitude marked by stupor, eyes that cannot see, and ears that cannot hear, even to this very day."*c* 9And David says, "Let their table become a snare and a hunting net, their death-trap trigger, and their retribution. 10 Let their eyes be darkened so they cannot see, and their back bent down continually."*d*

11Now what? The only result of their stumbling was not that they fell, was it? Certainly not! On the contrary, their falling aside [was made the occasion of] salvation for the Gentiles, and should incite [the Jews] to seek a similar blessing.*e* 12Now if their falling aside [contributed to] the enrichment of the world, and their defection [contributed to] the enrichment of the Gentiles, how much more their fulfillment!

13Now I say to you who are Gentiles: Inasmuch as I myself am an apostle to the Gentiles, I seek to accomplish the utmost through my ministry, 14hoping by this means to stir to jealous rivalry my own kinsmen and [thus] to save some of them. 15For if their rejection [has resulted in] the reconciliation of the world, what would their reception [mean] but life from the dead? 16If the first portion of dough is holy, so also is the entire lump. And if the root is holy, so also are the branches.

17Now if some of the branches were broken off, and you, being [of the stock of] a wild olive tree, were grafted in among them, and have become a partaker of the rich sap of the [cultivated] olive's

---

*a*1 Kings 19:10.
*b*1 Kings 19:18.
*d*Ps. 69:22-23.
*c*Isa. 29:10; Deut. 29:4.
*e*Literally, *incite them to jealousy*, or *to envious rivalry*.

root, [18]do not be boasting against the branches. But if you are inclined to feel superior, [bear in mind that] you do not support the root, but the root supports you. [19]You will reply, Branches were broken off so that I on my part might be grafted in! [20]Not exactly. They were broken off because of unbelief, and [it is only] by faith that you yourself remain standing. Stop being conceited, but maintain an attitude of reverential fear.[f] [21]For if God did not spare the natural branches, he certainly will not spare you.

[22]Therefore you should be aware of the kindness and the sternness of God—upon those who have fallen, sternness; but upon you, his kindness, if you continue [to trust] in that kindness. Otherwise, you too will be cut off. [23]And even the others, if they do not remain in their unbelief, will be grafted in. For God is able to graft them in again. [24]For if you were cut out from an essentially wild olive tree and, contrary to nature, you were grafted into a cultivated olive tree, how much easier it should be to graft these natural [branches] into their own olive tree!

[25]To prevent you from too much presumption, [my] brothers, I want you to understand this revealed secret: hardening in the case of many has come upon Israel and it will continue until the fulfillment of the Gentiles takes place. [26]And in this manner all Israel[g] will be saved, just as it stands written, "From out of Zion the Deliverer will come. He will turn ungodliness away from Jacob. [27]And this is my covenant with them, when I take away their sins."[h]

[28]From the standpoint of the gospel, [the Jews] are enemies for your sake. But from the standpoint of [God's] original selection, they are beloved on account of their forefathers. [29]For God is not subject to regret with regard to his gracious gifts and his call. [30]Even as you once were disobedient to God, but now have been shown mercy on the occasion of their disobedience, [31]thus they also now have disobeyed on the occasion of the mercy shown you, in order that they too may now be shown mercy. [32]For God has shut up together [in one category] all men because of [their] disobedience, so that he might show mercy to them all.

---

[f]Or, be afraid [of falling away through unbelief].

[g]Spiritual Israel. In this Epistle, Paul uses Israel in a dual sense, e.g. 2:28-29; 9:6-8.

[h]Isa. 59:20-21. Paul quotes loosely from the Septuagint. The Hebrew of Isa. 59:20 brings out clearly the fact that repentance on the part of Israel is a prerequisite to God's forgiveness and blessing. See the rendering of the Hebrew in the Authorized, English Revised, and Revised Standard Versions.

33O the depth of the riches and of the wisdom and of the knowledge of God![i] How unsearchable [are] his decisions, and how inscrutable his ways! 34"For who has ever comprehended the Lord's thoughts? Or who has ever become his counsellor? 35Or who has ever first given God anything, and thus put God under obligation to pay him back?"[j] 36Because all things have their origin in him, and exist through him, and are for him! To him be glory forever! Amen.

Chapter 12

Therefore I exhort you, [my] brothers, in view of the compassions of God, to present completely your entire selves[a] as a living sacrifice, holy and well-pleasing to God, for this is your reasonable service. 2Do not let this age be setting the pattern for your behavior, but continue being transformed by the renewing of your thinking powers, so that you keep discerning what is God's will—[what is] good and well-pleasing and complete.

3Through the divine favor having been given to me, I ask every person among you not to overestimate himself [or his abilities], but to cultivate an attitude of discretion in accordance with the measure of faith which God has apportioned to each one.

4For just as there are many parts in one [human] body, and all the parts do not have the same function, 5so we, who are many [believers], are one body in Christ, and we are individually members of each other. 6Now we have [certain] gifts that differ according to the divine favor which has been granted to us. [Let each recipient render proper service in the field in which he is qualified.] If [one's gift is] prophecy, [let it be exercised] according to the proportion of his faith[b] 7If it is service, [let it be exercised] in service. If it is teaching, [let it be exercised] in teaching. 8If it is exhortation, [let it be exercised] in exhortation. The one who shares [material things should do so] with liberality. The one who presides [should do so] with enthusiasm. The one who renders deeds of kindness [should do so] with cheerfulness.

---

iOr, O the depth of the riches, both of the wisdom and of the knowledge of God!
jIsa. 40:13; Job 35:7; 41:11.   aLiterally, *your bodies*.
bOr, in agreement with the faith.

⁹[There must be absolutely] no hypocrisy with regard to love. Constantly abhor that which is wicked. Always cling to the good. ¹⁰Be devoted to one another in brotherly love, [as members of the same family]. Take the lead in giving honor to each other. ¹¹Never let up in zeal. Keep on fire with the Spirit. Be constantly devoted to the service of the Lord, ¹²rejoicing in hope, patient in hardship, steadfastly continuing in prayer, ¹³sharing with the saints who are in need, always practicing hospitality.

¹⁴ Seek the best interests of those who persecute you. Strive for their well-being, and do not invoke evil [upon them]. ¹⁵Rejoice with persons who rejoice, and weep with persons who weep. ¹⁶Cultivate the attitude of mutual understanding for each other. Do not be haughty, but associate yourselves with the humble. Do not become self-opinionated.

¹⁷Never return evil for evil to anyone. Take careful forethought [about your conduct]. Let it be proper in the presence of everyone. ¹⁸If possible, as far as the responsibility is yours, to be at peace with everybody. ¹⁹Do not avenge yourselves, beloved, but leave place for [God's] wrath, for it stands written, " 'Vengeance belongs to me; I myself will pay [them] back,' saith the Lord."ᶜ ²⁰So [as opposed to seeking revenge], if your enemy is hungry, give him food. If he is thirsty, give him something to drink. For by such action, you may induce him to repent.ᵈ ²¹Never allow any evil person or thingᵉ to overcome you, but keep overcoming the evil by means of the good.

Chapter 13

Let every individual be submissive to the ruling [civil] authorities. For there is no authority except by [the sanction of] God, and the existing [authorities] stand established by him. ²Consequently he who sets himself against the authoritiesᵃ has reached a state of resistance against God's arrangement. And those who have reached such a state of resistance will receive judgment upon themselves.

ᶜDeut. 32:35.   ᵈLiterally, *you will heap coals of fire on his head*.
ᵉ*Kakou, evil,* here is either masculine or neuter. Its second use in this verse is neuter.
ᵃThe Greek is singular because Paul states a principle.

³For rulers [as a class^b] are not a terror to good conduct but to evil. Now do you wish to have no fear of the authority? Practice doing good, and you will receive commendation from it. ⁴For it is God's agent for your good. But if you are an evil doer, [you have reason to] be afraid. For it is not for nothing that he bears the sword. In fact, he is an instrument of divine order to inflict God's wrath upon the one who practices evil.

⁵So you must remain in subjection, not only to avoid this wrath, but also for the sake of conscience. ⁶This is why you pay taxes, for public officials are [servants] of God [in] steadily giving their energies to this ministration.^c ⁷Pay them all that which is due to them—taxes to the [collector of] taxes, revenue to the [collector of] revenue, respect to whom respect [is due], honor to whom honor [is due].

⁸Owe no one anything, except the purposive good will [patterned after the example of Christ] which is our perpetual^d debt to each other. He who continues demonstrating this good will to his fellowmen is in the state of having fully met the requirements of [the entire category of] law. ⁹For [the commandments], You must not commit adultery, You must not kill, You must not steal, You must not have evil desire, and whatever other command of a different kind there may be—all are summed up in this principle: You must love your neighbor as yourself. ¹⁰This purposive good will does not work any harm to its neighbor. Therefore, it is the fulfillment [of everything in the whole realm] of law.

¹¹And let us live like this, realizing the significance of the time period, that it is already the hour for you to be aroused from sleep. For now is our [ultimate] salvation nearer than when we became believers. ¹²The night has almost ended. The day has drawn near. So let us thoroughly and completely put away from ourselves the deeds of darkness, and let us once and for all put on the full equipment of the light.

¹³Let us conduct ourselves honorably, as in the day, not indulging in revellings and drunken sprees, not in illicit sexual intimacies and excesses like people who have lost their sense of shame, [and] not in contention and jealousy. ¹⁴Instead, be clothed with the Lord Jesus Christ, and make no plans for expressing any desires of the old nature.

---

^b Denoted by the Greek article.   ^c Literally, *to this very thing.*
^d Implied by the present infinitive of *agapaō.* The cognate noun is *agapē,* the sacrificial, redemptive love revealed in Christ.

Chapter 14

Now make it a practice to receive to yourselves the person whose faith is weak [because of lack of moral discernment], but not for the purpose of arguing about opinions. ²One man has sufficient confidence to eat any kind of food.ᵃ Another, being over-scrupulous, eats [only] vegetables. ³Let the man who eats [any kind of food] stop treating with contempt the man who abstains. And let the one who abstains stop criticizing the one who eats, for God has fully received him.ᵇ ⁴Just who are you to be judging a servant of someone else? To his own lord he stands or falls. But he will be made to stand, for the Lord is able to make him stand.

⁵One person considers a [certain] day more important than another day. Someone else considers every day alike. Let each individual be fully assured in his own mind. ⁶He who esteems the day esteems it to the Lord. He who eats [any kind of food] does so to the Lord, for he gives thanks to God. And he who abstains does so to the Lord, and he gives thanks to God. ⁷Indeed, no one of us lives to himself, and no one dies to himself. ⁸If we live, we live to the Lord. And if we die, we die to the Lord. So whether we live or whether we die, we belong to the Lord. ⁹This is why Christ died and came to life, that he might become Lord of both the dead and the living.

¹⁰Why, then, do youᶜ [the scrupulous personᵈ] go on criticizing your brother? Or also why do you [the unscrupulous person] continue treating your brother with contempt? Actually we must all appear before the judgment seat of God. ¹¹For it stands written, " 'As surely as I live' declares the Lord, 'before me every knee shall bend, and every tongue shall make full acknowledgment to God."ᶜ ¹²This means that each one of us will have to answer for himself to God.

¹³Therefore let us cease the habit of passing judgment on one another. Instead, make it your permanent determinationᶠ not to be setting up anything of the character of a stumbling block or a snare for your brother. ¹⁴I know and stand persuaded in the Lord Jesus that nothing is unclean in itself. It is unclean only to the individual

---

ᵃLiterally, *all things*.
ᵇOr, received him [unto Himself].
ᶜEmphatic by personal pronoun and its position in the Greek sentence.
ᵈIndicated by verse 3.   ᶜIsa. 45:23.
ᶠLiterally, *judge once for all* (aorist imperative).

who regards it as unclean. [15]If your brother is grieved because of some food you eat, you are no longer acting according to [the norm of] purposive good will.[g]

Stop destroying, by means of what you eat, that person in whose behalf Christ died! [16]You[h] have the [supreme] good. Let it not be slandered. [17]Indeed the kingdom of God is not [a matter of] eating and drinking, but [it is] righteousness and peace and joy in the Holy Spirit. [18]Certainly whoever in this way serves the Christ is well pleasing to God and is of tested worth before men.

[19]Accordingly, therefore, we are pursuing[i] the things of peace and the things that promote mutual upbuilding. [20]Stop tearing down[j] God's work for the sake of food! All things [classified as food] are indeed [ceremonially] clean. But [anything] is bad for the man who is a stumbling block by what he eats. [21]The expedient course is not to eat meat, nor to drink wine, nor [to do] anything that causes your brother to stumble.[k]

[22]In this regard, keep your confidence as a personal matter between God and yourself. Truly happy is the man who does not condemn himself in what he tests and approves. [23]But the man who hesitates in uncertainty stands condemned if he eats, because [his action] is not based on confidence, and any [action] not based on confidence is sin.

Chapter 15

Now we who are strong [in matters of conscience] ought[a] to bear the weaknesses of those who are not strong, and not to go on pleasing ourselves. [2]Let each one of us try to please his neighbor with regard to the good, with a view to [his] spiritual advancement. [3]Most certainly the Christ did not please himself, but as it stands written [of him], "The reproaches of those who reproach thee have fallen upon me."[b]

---

gAgapē.   hPlural, which seems to denote the whole church.
iSome manuscripts have present subjunctive, Let us pursue.
jThe imperative is singular, indicating that a particular group is addressed.
kCf. 1 Cor. 8:1ff.
aOpheilomen, we are under obligation, is placed first in the sentence for emphasis.
bPs. 69:9.

[4]All the things previously written were recorded for our instruction, in order that through perseverance and through the encouragement which the Scriptures give[c] we might maintain our hope. [5]Now may God, who is the source of this perseverance and of this encouragement, grant you constant unanimity of thought in accordance with [the standard revealed in] Christ Jesus, [6]so that with oneness of purpose in one voice you may continue glorifying the God and Father of our Lord Jesus Christ.

[7]Therefore, have the habit of receiving each other to yourselves, even as also the Christ has received us[d] to himself for the glory of God. [8]What I mean is that Christ stands constituted a minister to the circumcised to vindicate God's truthfulness by fulfilling the promises made to the fathers, [9]and that the Gentiles might glorify God on account of his mercy, just as it stands written, "Therefore I will fully confess thee among the Gentiles. And to the accompaniment of a stringed instrument I will sing praises to thy name."[e] [10]And again it declares, "Rejoice, O Gentiles, with his people!"[f] [11]And again, "Praise the Lord, all the Gentiles. Yea, let all peoples extol him!"[g] [12]And furthermore Isaiah declares, "The Descendant of Jesse will come, even he who rises up to rule the Gentiles. On him the Gentiles will place their hope."[h]

[13]Now may God, who is the source of this hope, fill you with all joy and peace as you go on exercising faith, so that you may be overflowing with this hope by the power of the Holy Spirit.

[14]I myself am fully confident regarding you, my brothers, that you yourselves are full of goodness, [that you are] in the state of having been filled with all [essential] knowledge, competent even to admonish one another. [15]But, just as an additional reminder to you, I have written rather boldly on some points[i] because of the gracious favor God has bestowed upon me [16]in appointing me a minister of Christ Jesus to the Gentiles. [Thus I am] engaged in the sacred service of the gospel of God, in order to bring about the presentation of the Gentiles as an acceptable offering—[an offering] in the state of having been sanctified by the Holy Spirit.

---

[c]Or, in order that through the perseverance which the Scriptures [induce in us] through the counsel which they [enjoin upon us] we might continue to have hope.
[d]Some manuscripts read *humas, you.*   [e]Ps. 18:49.
[f]Deut. 32:43.   [g]Ps. 117:1.   [h]Isa. 11:10.
[i]Or, in some parts [of this letter].

¹⁷Therefore I have [basis for] glorying in Christ Jesus concerning the things relating to [the service of] God. ¹⁸I will not presume to mention anything except that which Christ has accomplished through me for the purpose of bringing the Gentiles to obedience. ¹⁹[He wrought in me] by word and deed through the might of signs and wonders, by the power of the Holy Spirit; so that from Jerusalem and as far around as Illyricum, I have fulfilled with abiding results [my ministry in] the gospel of the Christ.

²⁰And in this manner it always has been my aim[j] to declare the good news where the name of Christ has never been heard, so as not to build upon a foundation laid by another workman, ²¹but as it stands written, "Those who have not been told about him will see, and those who have not heard will understand.[k]

²²This explains why I have so frequently been prevented by many responsibilities[l] from coming to you. ²³But now, as I no longer have a place [of work] in these regions, and as I have for a good many years cherished a longing to come to you, ²⁴I am hoping to see you when I pass through [Rome] on my way to Spain, and by you to be assisted on the journey there, after I have had the pleasure of your fellowship for a while.

²⁵However, at the present I am going to Jerusalem for the purpose of delivering the collection[m] to the saints. ²⁶For [the churches in] Macedonia and Achaia have resolved to contribute a certain sum for the poor among the saints at Jerusalem. ²⁷Indeed they were glad to do so, and actually the Gentiles[n] owe a debt to the Jews. For if the Gentiles have shared in their spiritual benefits, [the Gentiles] in fact ought to minister to them in material things. ²⁸After I have completed this [task], and have properly delivered the contribution, I shall proceed toward Spain and visit you on the way. ²⁹And I know that when I do reach you, I shall come in the fullness of Christ's blessing.

³⁰Now I appeal to you, [my] brothers, through our Lord Jesus Christ, and by the love[o] which the Spirit imparts, to agonize together with me in your prayers to God in my behalf, ³¹that I may be delivered from those persons in Judea who are disobedient, and that my service which takes me to Jerusalem may be well received by the

---

[j]Or, I consider it an honor.
[k]Isa. 52:15.   [l]Literally, *many things.*
[m]Literally, *ministering to the saints.* Cf. 1 Cor. 16:1-4; 2 Cor. 8:1ff; 9:1ff.
[n]Literally, *they are debtors of them.*   [o]*Agapē.*

saints; [32]so that, by the will of God, I may come to you with glad-
ness and enjoy [a period of] refreshing rest in your company. [33]May
the God of peace be with all of you! Amen.

Chapter 16

Now I commend to you our sister Phoebe, who is a servant[a] of the
church at Cenchreae. [2]Receive her in the Lord, in the manner in
which saints should welcome one another. Stand by her in whatever
matter she may have need of you, for indeed she on her part has
rendered much assistance to many, including myself.

[3]Give my greetings to Prisca and Aquila, my fellow workers in
Christ Jesus. [4]They once risked their own lives in behalf of mine.
Not only I but also all the churches of the Gentiles give thanks to
them. [5][Greet], too, the church which meets in their house. Greet
my beloved Epaenetus, who is the first convert won for Christ in
[the province of] Asia. [6]Greet Mary, who has toiled a great deal for
you. [7]Greet Andronicus and Junias, my fellow countrymen, who also
shared imprisonment with me. They are men of esteem among the
apostles, and they have been in Christ longer than I.

[8]Greet Ampliatus, my beloved in the Lord. [9]Give my greetings to
Urbanus, our fellow worker in Christ, and to my beloved Stachys.
[10]Greet Apelles, that man of tested character in [the work of] Christ.
Greet those of the [household] of Aristobulus. [11]Greet Herodion, my
fellow countryman. Greet those of the [household] of Narcissus who
are in the Lord. [12]Greet Tryphaena and Tryphosa, those diligent
toilers in [the cause of] the Lord. Greet Persis, the beloved lady who,
with regard to many things, has worked hard for the Lord.[b]

[13]Greet Rufus, that excellent man in the Lord; also his mother—
[she has been a mother] to me too. [14]Greet Asyncritus, Phlegon,
Hermes, Patrobas, Hermas, and the brothers who are associated with
them. [15]Greet Philologus and Julia, Nereus and his sister, and
Olympas and all the saints who are associated with them. [16]Greet
one another with a holy kiss. All the churches of the Christ send their
greetings to you.

---

[a]Or, deacon. The Greek word, *diakonos*, is common gender.
[b]Literally, *in the Lord.*

[17]Now I urge you, [my] brothers, to keep on the lookout for those persons who create divisions and means of entrapment. [Their teachings are] contrary to the doctrine which you have learned. [18]Keep away from them, for such men are not obedient to our Lord Christ, but to their own selfish appetite, and by means of their smooth speech and flattering style they deceive completely the hearts of the credulous.

[19]The report of your obedience [to the truth] has reached everyone. So I rejoice on account of you, yet I want you to be wise with reference to what is good, but untainted with reference to what is evil. [20]The God of peace will crush Satan under your feet swiftly. The gracious care of our Lord Jesus be with you!

[21]Timothy, my fellow worker, greets you, and [so do] Lucius and Jason and Sosipater, my fellow countrymen. [22](I, Tertius, the amanuensis[c] for this letter, greet you in the Lord.) [23]Gaius, my host, and [host] of the entire church, greets you. Erastus, the administrator[d] of the city, and Brother Quartus, greet you.

[25e]Now to him who is able to establish you in accord with the gospel as I preach it,[f] even the proclamation of Jesus Christ, in accord with the disclosure of the mystery which was kept in a state of silence during long ages, [26]but now has been made plain through prophetic scriptures, [and] by the command of the eternal God, made known to all the Gentiles to bring them to the obedience which faith impels—[27]to God who alone is wise, to whom through Jesus Christ be glory forever![g] Amen.

---

[c]Literally, *the one having written.*   [d]Or, treasurer.

[e]Nestle, following the best textual authorities, omits verse 24. But the benediction of the verse, almost word for word, is included in v. 20 by these sources.

[f]Literally, *my gospel.*   [g]Literally, *unto the ages of the ages.*

FIRST CORINTHIANS

Chapter 1

Paul, a called apostle of Christ Jesus by the will of God, and Sosthenes our[a] brother, [2]to which the church of God which is at Corinth, to those who are in the state of having been sanctified in Christ Jesus, called saints, along with all those who in every place call upon the name of our Lord Jesus Christ, who is their Lord as well as ours.[b] [3]Gracious favor be yours and peace from God our Father and the Lord Jesus Christ.

[4]I am always thanking God concerning you, because of the grace of God bestowed upon you in Christ Jesus, [5]that through him you have been enriched in every respect, with eloquence of speech and depth of insight.[c] [6]Thus the testimony [we gave] about Christ has been confirmed among you, [7]so that you have no lack of any spiritual endowment[d] while you are eagerly waiting for the return[e] of our Lord Jesus Christ. [8]He will sustain you until the end, [that you may be] blameless in the Day of our Lord Jesus Christ. [9]God is faithful, and by him you were called into fellowship with his Son, Jesus Christ our Lord.

[10]Now I urge you, brothers, through the name of our Lord Jesus Christ, that you all maintain doctrinal agreement,[f] and that there be no factions among you, but that you may continue in the state of having been united in thought and in judgment.[g] [11]For it has been reported to me, my brothers, by members of Chloe's household, that there are dissentions among you.

[12]What I mean is, that one of you says, "I indeed am of Paul;" another, "I am of Apollos;" another, "I am of Cephas;" another, "I am of Christ." [13]Has Christ been divided? Paul was not crucified for

---

[a]Literally, *the.*   [b]Literally, *theirs and ours.*
[c]Literally, *with all speech and with all knowledge.*
[d]Or, spiritual gift.   [e]Literally, *revelation.*
[f]Literally, *consistently speak the same thing.*
[g]Or, made complete in the same mind and in the same purpose.

43

you, was he? Or were you baptized to indicate the commitment of your lives to Paul?[h] [14]I am thankful that I baptized none of you except Crispus and Gaius. [15]So no one can say that you were baptized to indicate devotion to me.[i] [16][On second thought] I did baptize the household of Stephanus too. In addition to these, I cannot recall that I baptized anyone else. [17]For Christ did not send me to baptize, but to preach the gospel; [and to proclaim it] not with clever speech, lest the cross of Christ be robbed of its potency.

[18]Actually the message about the cross is foolishness to those who are perishing, but to us who are being saved it is the power of God. [19]For it stands written, "I will destroy the wisdom of the wise, and I will set aside the subtlety of the subtle."[j] [20]Where is the learned man? Where is the expositor?[k] Where is the disputant of this present age? Has not God turned human wisdom into folly? [21]For since in God's providence the world never came to know God through its wisdom, it pleased God through the "foolishness" of what we preach[l] to save those who believe. [22]The Jews demand miracles, and the Greeks pursue wisdom. [23]But we preach Christ crucified,[m] an obstacle of stumbling[n] to Jews and foolishness to Gentiles. [24]But to those who have heard and obeyed [God's] call,[o] both Jews and Greeks, Christ [is] the power of God and the wisdom of God. [25]For that act of God [which the world regards as] foolish is wiser than men, and that act of God [which the world regards as] weak is stronger than men.

[26]Now think about your calling, brothers. Not many [of you were] wise according to human opinion. Not many [were] influential. Not many [were] of noble birth. [27]But God especially chose[p] the foolish things of the world in order that he might put to shame its wise men. And God especially chose[p] the weak things of the world in order that he might put to shame its strong things. [28]And God especially chose[p] the insignificant and useless things of the world—the things that are not[q]—in order that he might render ineffective the things that are,

---

[h]Literally, *baptized into the name of Paul?*
[i]Literally, *baptized into my name.*
[j]Cf. Isa. 29:14.　　　[k]Literally, *the scribe* (the Jewish interpreter of the Law).
[l]Literally, *of the proclamation.*
[m]The perfect passive participle, *estaurōmenon,* emphasizes the permanent results of Christ's crucifixion, i.e., he was and remains the Savior.
[n]Literally, *a snare,* or *the trigger that springs a trap.*　　　[o]Cf. footnote on Rom. 8:28.
[p]Or, God *selected for himself, exelexato,* aorist middle indicative.
[q]Paul seems to refer to individuals who were of such humble background that the world regarded them as nonentities or mere nothings.

[29]so that no human being may ever boast in his sight. [30]But you are his children[r] through Christ Jesus, who by God's will[s] became for us wisdom and righteousness and sanctification and redemption. [31]Thus it stands written, "He that boasts, let him boast in the Lord."[t]

Chapter 2

When I came to you, brothers, I did not come with speculative ideas or unusual eloquence, announcing to you the testimony of God. [2]Indeed, I determined to know nothing among you except Jesus Christ —and this One as crucified.[a] [3]And I approached you in weakness and with much anxiety and timidity. [4]And my speech and my message [were] not in eloquent words of sophistry, but in demonstration of the Spirit and of power, [5]in order that your faith might not rest on man's wisdom but on God's power.

[6]However [there is] a wisdom that we speak among the mature, but [it is] a wisdom not of the present age nor of the rulers of the present age, who are in the process of being overthrown. [7]But we speak God's mysterious wisdom—the [wisdom] long kept hidden [but now revealed[b]]—which God planned before the ages with a view to our glory. [8]None of the rulers of the present age has discerned [this wisdom]. For if they had come to know it, they would not have crucified the Lord of glory. [9]Just as it stands written, "Things which eye has not seen, nor ear heard, and which have not entered the heart of man—All this God has prepared for those who love him."[c] [10]But God has revealed [these things] to us through the Spirit; for the Spirit explores everything, even the deep things of God. [11]Now who among men knows a man's thoughts except the man's own spirit within him? Even so, no one has perceived God's thoughts except the Spirit of God. [12]We have not received the spirit of the world, but the Spirit that is from God, so that we may know the things which God has freely given to us. [13]And these truths[d] we declare, not in

---

[r]Literally, *But you are of him.*
[s]Literally, *who became wisdom to us from God.*   [t]Cf. Jer. 9:23f.
[a]Cf. note on 1:23.

[b]The Greek noun *mustērion, mystery,* often designates truth once hidden but now revealed, namely, God's redemptive purpose in Christ. Cf. Rom. 16:25-26; Eph. 1:9; 3:3ff.; 6:19; Col. 1:26-27; 4:3; 1 Tim. 3:16.   [c]Cf. Isa. 64:4.

[d]Literally, *these things.*

words taught by human wisdom but in [words] taught by the Spirit, expressing spiritual ideas with spiritual words.[e]

14Now a man with a natural insight does not receive the things of the Spirit of God, for they are foolishness to him, and he is not able to grasp [them] because they are spiritually discerned. 15But the man with spiritual insight discerns everything, yet he himself is discerned by no one. 16For "who ever came to know the mind of the Lord so as to be able to instruct him?"[f] But we have the mind of Christ.

Chapter 3

As for me, brothers, I could not talk to you as to spiritually minded men, but as to persons with carnal tendencies, as to babes in Christ. 2I fed you milk, not solid food, for you were not able [to receive solid food]. In fact, even now you are not strong enough [for it] 3because you are still prompted by low motives. For where there is jealousy and strife among you, are you not prompted by low motives and acting like ordinary people? 4When one says, "I indeed am of Paul," and another, "I am of Apollos," are you not thinking merely from a human standpoint?[a]

5Actually what is Apollos? And what is Paul? Only ministers through whom you came to believe, even as the Lord gave to each [minister the ability to perform his task].[b] 6I planted [the gospel among you]. Apollos watered [it]. But God made it grow. 7So neither the planter nor the waterer counts for much,[c] but [the preeminence belongs to] God who causes the growth. 8The planter and the waterer contribute to the same endeavor,[d] and each will receive his own reward in proportion to his own service. 9For we are fellow workers [in the service] of God. You are a field which God is cultivating. [Or, to change the metaphor,] you are a building which God is constructing.

10In carrying out my commission,[e] like a competent architect I have laid a foundation, and someone else builds upon it. But let each one be careful how he builds. 11The foundation is already laid—it is

---

eOr, interpreting spiritual things to spiritual persons.   fCf. Isa. 40:13.
aLiterally, *are you not* [mere] *men?*
bOr, even as the Lord gave [grace] to each [of you].
cLiterally, *is anything.*   dLiterally, *are one thing.*
eLiterally, *According to God's grace given to me.*

Jesus Christ—and no man can lay any other. [12]Now upon this foundation others will build with gold, silver, or costly stones, [or with] wood, grass, or straw.

[13]And the work of each builder will become evident, for the [judgment] Day will disclose it because [that Day] is [to be] revealed with fire, and the fire will test each man's work and will show what sort it is. [14]If what a man built endures, he will receive a reward. [15]If any man's work burns down, he will suffer loss but he himself will be saved like a person barely escaping from a raging fire.[f]

[16]You know, do you not, that you are God's sanctuary, and that God's Spirit dwells in you? [17]If anyone destroys God's sanctuary, God will destroy him. For God's sanctuary is holy, and you yourselves, by your very character, are that sanctuary.

[18]Let no one deceive himself. If any of you imagines that he is wise with the [wisdom of] this age, let him become "foolish" in order that he may become wise. [19]For the wisdom of this world is folly in God's sight. Indeed the Scripture tells about[g] "the One who catches the wise in their cunning."[h] [20]And [it says] again, "The Lord knows the reasonings of the arrogant, that they are futile."[i]

[21]So let no one boast about men. Actually everything belongs to you—[22]Paul, Apollos, and Cephas; the world, life, and death; things present and things to come—all things are yours! [23]And you belong to Christ, and Christ belongs to God!

Chapter 4

Consequently, let us be regarded as Christ's assistants and stewards of the mysteries[a] of God. [2]Furthermore, in this matter of stewards, it is required that a person be found trustworthy. [3]Now to me, it is a very small matter to be examined by you, or by any human tribunal. Actually I do not [assume the right to] examine myself. [4]Although I know nothing against myself, this does not mean that I stand acquitted, for the One who examines me is the Lord. [5]So do not

fLiterally, *saved as through fire.*
gLiterally, *Indeed it stands written.*
hCf. Job 5:13.   iCf. Ps. 94:11.
aSecret truths revealed through the gospel. Cf. 2:7.

be passing judgment before the [proper] time, [but wait] until the Lord comes. He will bring to light what is now hidden in darkness, and he will reveal the motives of men's hearts. Then each man will receive from God whatever recognition is appropriate.

6Now these things, brothers, I have applied figuratively to myself and to Apollos for your benefit in order that from our example[b] you may learn the [principle], "Go not beyond what stands written," that none of you may make inflated claims on behalf of one [leader] against another. 7Who makes you superior to others?[c] And what have you that did not come to you as a gift?[d] And if indeed it was bestowed as a gift,[e] why are you boasting as though you deserved it?[f]

8So you have already reached a state of completion![g] You have already become rich! Without us you have begun to reign! I certainly wish that you did reign, so that we could reign with you! 9As a matter of fact, it seems to me that God has set us, his apostles, in the lowest category of all, like men sentenced to die.[h] For we have become an exhibition to the world, both to angels and to men. 10We are fools for Christ's sake, but you are wise in Christ! We are weak, but you are strong! You are held in honor, but we are despised!

11Until the present moment we are hungry and thirsty. We are scantily clothed. We are kicked about. We are homeless. 12We toil continually, earning our living[i] with our own hands. When we are reviled, we bless. When we are persecuted, we do not retaliate.[j] 13When we are slandered, we do not reply in kind.[k] Until now we are regarded as the rubbish of the world, the offscouring of society.[l]

14I am not writing these things to shame you, but to admonish you as my beloved children. 15You might have ten thousand guardians[m] in Christ, but you can have only one father. As a matter of fact, I myself begot you in Christ Jesus by bringing you the gospel. 16Therefore I urge you, follow my example. 17With this in mind, I

---

[b]Literally, *in order that in us,* or *through us you may learn.*

[c]Literally, *Who distinguishes you?*

[d]Literally, *And what have you that you did not receive?*

[e]Literally, *And if indeed you received* [it].

[f]Literally, *as though you did not receive* [it]?

[g]Paul is speaking ironically to combat the unwarranted pride of his readers.

[h]Or, last in the procession, like captives doomed to die in the arena. The metaphor is drawn from a victorious general's march of triumph.

[i]Literally, *working.*   [j]Literally, *we bear up* [under it].

[k]Or, we respond with [gentle] appeal.   [l]Literally, *of all things,* or *of all men.*

[m]Cf. Gal. 3:24, 25.

am sending[n] Timothy to you. As my beloved and faithful son[o] in the Lord, he will remind you of my ways in Christ Jesus, exactly as I teach everywhere in every church. [18]Some of you have become arrogant, assuming that I am not coming to [visit] you. [19]But I shall come to you soon, if the Lord wills, and I shall find out, not how much the arrogant ones talk, but how much they have accomplished. [20]For the kingdom of God is not a matter of talk, but of constructive action. [21]What is your choice? Shall I come to you with a rod, or with love in a spirit of tenderness?

Chapter 5

It is actually reported that there is immorality among you, and immorality of a kind that is not practiced even among pagans[a]—that a man is carrying on an incestuous relationship with his father's wife. [2]And are you complacent [about this matter], instead of grieving over it and removing from your midst the one who has done such a thing? [3]For my part, although I am absent in body, [I am] present in spirit, and thus present I have already passed judgment on the offender.

[4]When you have assembled in the name of the Lord Jesus, and by my apostolic authority,[b] then with the power of our Lord Jesus [5]the guilty one is to be handed over to Satan. This discipline may cause him [to repent and overcome his sinful desires] so that his spirit may be saved in the Day of the Lord.

[6]Your complacency[c] is not good. You know, do you not, that a small amount of leaven affects all the dough? [7]Cleanse out the old leaven, in order that you may be a new society in conformity with your status as believers.[d] For indeed our Passover Lamb—Christ— has been sacrificed. [8]Therefore let us keep celebrating the festival [of our faith], not with any old leaven, nor with leaven of malice and vice, but with the unleavened loaves of purity and truth.

---

[n]Epistolary aorist, by which a writer views his letter from the point of time of its recipients. [o]Greek, *teknon, child,* a term of endearment.
[a]Incest was forbidden by Greek and Roman law. For Jewish law, cf. Lev. 18:6-18; 20:11-21; Deut. 27:20ff. [b]Literally, *and of my spirit.*
[c]Or, boasting. [d]Literally, *as you are unleavened.*

[9]I wrote to you in my letter[e] not to associate intimately with immoral people. [10]I did not mean that you were to have no contact whatsoever with the immoral people of this world, or with the covetous and extortioners or idolaters, for in that case you would have to depart out of the world.

[11]But I meant[f] that you are not to associate intimately with any so-called brother who is an immoral or covetous man, or an idolater or a reviler or a drunkard or an extortioner—do not live on familiar terms with such a person.[g] [12]What business have I to judge the outsiders? It is your responsibility to judge those who are within [the congregation], is it not? [13]God will judge the outsiders. Remove the wicked person from among you at once!

Chapter 6

If any one of you has a dispute with a fellow believer, does he dare go to law before the unrighteous and not before the saints? [2]Do you not know that the saints will judge the world? And if the world is to be judged by you, are you incompetent to settle the most trivial problems? [3]Do you not know that we are to judge angels? How much more, then, should we resolve the affairs of this life!

[4]So if you have matters of this life to decide, why do you refer them to the judgment of people who are not esteemed by the church?[a] [5]I say this to your shame. Is there really no one among you who is competent enough to decide a matter between one brother and another? [6]Must brother take civil action against brother,[b] and that before unbelievers?

[7]Now the very fact that you have lawsuits with one another at all is an utter failure on your part. Why not rather submit to injustice? Why not rather let yourselves be defrauded? [8]Instead, you yourselves are practicing injustice and fraud—brother against brother!

[9]You know, do you not, that wrongdoers will not inherit the kingdom of God? Do not be deceived. Neither fornicators, nor idolaters, nor adulterers, nor lewd persons, nor homosexuals, [10]nor thieves, nor

---

[e]A former letter, not now extant.　　　　[f]Literally, *But now I write to you.*
[g]Literally, *not even to eat with such a man.*
[a]Or, then refer them to the judgment of those who are the least esteemed in the church.
[b]Literally, *But brother is judged against brother.*

covetous persons, nor drunkards, nor those who use abusive language, nor extortioners will inherit the kingdom of God. [11]Some of you used to be people like that.[c] But you have been washed clean. You have been sanctified. You have been brought into right standing [with God] in the name of the Lord Jesus Christ and by the Spirit of our God.

[12]Someone may say, "All things are permissible for me." But not all things are beneficial. He may insist, "All things are permissible for me." But I will not allow myself to be enslaved by anything. [13]It may be argued, "Foods are for the stomach, and the stomach is for foods." But God will eventually destroy both the one and the other. The body is not intended for immorality but for serving the Lord, and he is the Lord of the body.[d]

[14]God raised up the Lord and he will also raise us up by his power. [15]You know, do you not, that your bodies are members of Christ? Shall I then take the members of Christ, and make them members of a harlot? Absolutely not! [16]You know, do you not, that a man who joins himself to a harlot becomes one body with her? For the Scripture says,[e] "The two shall become one flesh."[f] [17]But he who is united to the Lord becomes one spirit with him.

[18]Always flee from sexual sin. Every [other] sin that a man may commit has an effect relatively external to his body,[g] but the man who commits fornication sins directly against his own body. [19]Or do you not know that your body is a sanctuary of the Holy Spirit who is in you—[the Spirit] whom you have [received] from God—and that you do not belong to yourselves? [20]Indeed, you were bought with a price! Then honor God with your body.

Chapter 7

Now let me consider the questions raised in your letter. It may be expedient for a man to remain unmarried. [2]But as a safeguard against immorality, let each man have a wife of his own, and each woman a husband of her own. [3]The husband should fulfill his obligations to his wife, and likewise also the wife [should fulfill her obligations] to

---

[c]Literally, *And these things some of you were.*
[d]Literally, *and the Lord is for the body.*   [e]Literally, *For it says,* or *He says.*
[f]Cf. Gen. 2:24.   [g]Literally, *is outside the body.*

her husband. [4]The wife does not have complete say regarding her own person but the husband [must be considered].

Likewise, the husband does not have complete say regarding his own person but the wife [must be considered]. [5]Do not deprive each other, unless it is only for a time and by mutual consent, in order that you may have adequate opportunity for prayer. Then come together again, to prevent Satan from tempting you on account of your lack of self-control. [6]I offer this advice by way of concession, not by command. [7]My personal preference would be that everyone were like myself. Nevertheless each of us has his own special gift from God, one to live in one way, another to live in a different way.

[8]To the unmarried and to the widows, I say that it is well for them to remain [single] as I am. [9]However, if they cannot exercise self-control, let them marry. For it is better to marry than to burn with sexual desire.

[10]To those who are already married I give command (not I myself but the Lord[a]): a wife is not to leave her husband. [11]But if she does leave him, let her either remain unmarried or be reconciled to her husband. And a husband is not to divorce his wife.

[12]To the others,[b] I give my own opinion (I have no precept from the Lord on this point[c]). If any brother has a wife who is not a believer, and she is willing to go on living with him, let him not divorce her. [13]And if a woman has a husband who is not a believer, and he is willing to go on living with her, let her not divorce her husband. [14]For the unbelieving husband is sanctified through [his relation to] the [believing] wife; and the unbelieving wife is sanctified through [her relation to] the believing husband.[d] Otherwise your children would be unclean, but now they are holy.

[15]If, however, the unbelieving spouse is determined to separate, let the separation take place. The brother or the sister does not remain bound in such cases. But God has called you[e] to peace. [16]How do you know, wife, whether or not you can save your husband? Or how do you know, husband, whether or not you can save your wife?

[a]Cf. Mark 10:11-12.

[b]Here Paul seems to refer to couples who were married before becoming believers.

[c]Paul knows of no traditional pronouncement of Jesus on this particular subject.

[d]The marriage union is sanctified. That is, it is legitimate, as the latter part of the verse shows.　　　[e]Some manuscripts read *hēmas, us*.

¹⁷But as a general rule, in accord with the Lord's appointment for each person, let each one continue to live in the status in which he was when God's call came to him. This is the principle which I emphasize*f* in all the churches. ¹⁸Was anyone called after he had been circumcised? He should not attempt to obliterate the mark of circumcision. Was anyone called when he was not circumcised? He should not receive circumcision. ¹⁹Neither circumcision nor uncircumcision has any merit, but what really counts is keeping God's commandments. ²⁰Let each person remain in the status in which he was when God called him.

²¹Were you a slave when you were called? Do not worry about it. Of course if you have the opportunity to become free, take advantage of it. ²²The slave who has been called by the Lord is a freedman of the Lord. On the other hand, the free man who has been called is a slave of Christ. ²³You were bought with a price. Do not become slaves of men. ²⁴So, brothers, in whatever [condition of life] each one was when he was called, in that status let him remain with God.

²⁵Now concerning the virgins, I have no instructions from the Lord,*g* but I offer you my considered opinion as a man who, through God's mercy, deserves your confidence.*h* ²⁶I think that, in view of the present difficult circumstances, it may be expedient—and probably is better—for a person to remain as he is. ²⁷Are you bound to a wife? Do not seek release. Are you unmarried? Do not seek a wife. ²⁸But if you do marry, you commit no sin. And if a girl marries, she commits no sin. However, people who marry*i* will have trouble in their outward affairs [due to the stress that is upon us*j*], and I am trying to spare you [that].

²⁹But bear in mind, brothers, that the appointed time has grown short. From now on [we should not consider any earthly relationship as permanent]. Let those who have wives not center their interests in wedlock. ³⁰Let those who weep live as though they had no time for sorrow, those who are glad as though they had no time for gaiety, those who are buying as though they did not possess anything. ³¹And let those who are busy with material pursuits not become engrossed in them, for the present world order is passing away.

---

*f*Literally, *Thus I command.* *g*See note on v. 12.
*h*Or, has kept faithful. *i*Literally, *such ones.* *j*Cf. v. 26.

³²I want you to be free from distracting anxieties. An unmarried man is concerned about the Lord's cause, how he may please the Lord. ³³But a married man is concerned about temporal things, how he may please his wife, ³⁴and so his concerns are divided. An unmarried woman or girl is concerned about the Lord's cause, so that she may be holy in body and spirit. But a married woman is concerned about temporal things, how she may please her husband. ³⁵I am saying this for your own benefit, not to put any restriction upon you, but to promote good order so your devotion to the Lord may be constant and undistracted.

³⁶If a man thinks he is not treating his virgin daughter*k* properly, if she is of marriageable age and wishes to marry,*l* let him grant her request. He does not commit sin—let the marriage take place. ³⁷On the other hand, when a father*m* has the firm conviction [that a single life is best for his daughter], and is under no compulsion [from her inclinations], but is free to act as he prefers, and has decided in his own heart to keep his daughter unmarried, he does well. ³⁸So he who gives his daughter in marriage does well, and he who does not give [his daughter] in marriage does better.*n*

³⁹A wife remains bound to her husband as long as he lives; but if he dies, she is free to marry anyone she wishes, only in the Lord. ⁴⁰But in my opinion she is happier if she remains as she is. And I think that I, too, have the Spirit of God.

Chapter 8

Now with regard to meat left over from idol worship,*a* it is true that we all have some knowledge about it. Knowledge puffs [a person] up, while concern *b* for the well-being of others builds [him] up. ²If anyone supposes that he has come into complete knowledge,

*k*The verb *gamizō, to give in marriage* (v. 38) shows that in this passage Paul is writing about the duty of a father toward a daughter of marriageable age.

*l*Literally, *and thus it ought to be.*

*m*Literally, *he who.*

*n*Not morally better, but more expedient due to the exigencies of the times.

*a*The portions of sacrificial animals not consumed on the pagan altars were eaten at feasts in the temples, or used for food in private homes, or sold in the markets. The use of such meat was often involved in the social relations of Christians with their heathen neighbors (cf. chap. 10:20-33).

*b*Greek, *agapē.*

he does not yet know as he ought to know. ³But if anyone loves God, he is known by him.ᶜ

⁴So, concerning eating meat previously associated with idol worship, we know that an idol has no actual existence in the world, and that there is no God but one. ⁵For even if other gods should exist either in heaven or on earth, even as there are many so-called gods and lords, ⁶yet for us there is only one God, the Father, who is the Source of all things, and for whom we live. And there is but one Lord, Jesus Christ, through whom are all things, and through whom we have our being.

⁷However, some people do not have this knowledge. There are those who, by force of habit,ᵈ still feel that in eating the meat in question they are participating in idol worship. And so their conscience, being oversensitive,ᵉ is disturbed. ⁸But food cannot bring us near to God. We lose nothing by not eating. We gain nothing by eating. ⁹Only make sure that your freedom does not become a hindrance to persons who are oversensitive.

¹⁰For if someone [who is weak in understanding] should see you, the possessor of knowledge, reclining at a dinner in an idol's temple, will not he, in violation of his conscience, be encouraged to eat the things sacrificed to idols? ¹¹So by your "knowledge" the oversensitive man—the brother for whom Christ died—is being ruined. ¹²By sinning like that against your brothers and smiting their weak conscience, you sin against Christ. ¹³Therefore, if what I eat causes my brother to stumble, I will never eat meat, to make sure that I do not cause my brother to stumble.

Chapter 9

Am I not free? Am I not an apostle? Have I not seen Jesus our Lord? Are you not yourselves proof of my work in the Lord? ²If I am not an apostle to others, I certainly am to you. For you yourselves [as believers] in the Lord are the seal which authenticates my apostleship. ³This is my reply to those who question my integrity.

⁴Have we not the right to receive material support [from those to whom we preach]? ⁵Have we not the right to take with us [on our

---

ᶜOr, that man is known (or approved) by Him.
ᵈOr, due to custom.　ᵉLiterally, *weak*.

travels] a wife who is a believer, as do the rest of the apostles, and the Lord's brothers, and Cephas? [6]Are Barnabas and I the only ones who have no right to be supported by the congregations among whom we work?[a] [7]Whoever serves as a soldier at his own expense? Who plants a vineyard and does not eat of its fruit? Or who shepherds a flock and does not drink from the milk of the flock? [8]I am not speaking from a purely human point of view, am I? Does not the Law also say these things? [9]Indeed, in the Law of Moses it stands written, "You shall not muzzle an ox while he is treading out the grain."[b]

Is it only for the oxen that God cares? [10]Or does he speak especially on our behalf? Indeed it was written mainly for our sake, because the plowman ought to plow, and the thresher [ought to thresh] in the expectation of sharing [in the harvest]. [11]Inasmuch as we have sown spiritual things among you, is it unreasonable[c] for us to reap material benefits from you? [12]If others share in the right of [being supported by] you, have not we [who first brought you the gospel[d]] a far greater [right to such support]?

However, we have not made use of this right, but we endure privations of every kind[e] to make sure that we do not hinder the gospel of Christ. [13]You know, do you not, that those who perform the temple rites receive their living from the temple, and those who serve at the altar receive a share of the gifts brought to the altar?[f] [14]According to the same principle, the Lord has directed that those who proclaim the gospel should get their living from the gospel.[g]

[15]But I, for my part, have not used any of these rights. Nor am I writing this now to secure financial support for myself. I would rather die than for anyone to deprive me of glorying [in the fact that I take nothing for my work]. [16]Even if I preach the gospel, I have no ground for boasting. For necessity compels me to do so. Woe to me if I fail to preach the gospel! [17]If I declare it willingly, I have a reward. But if unwillingly, it is still a responsibility entrusted to me. [18]Then what pay do I get? Just this: that in preaching the gospel I may present it without charge, so as not to take full advantage of my right to be supported by it.

---

[a]Literally, *to cease working* [for a living].   [b]Deut. 25:4.
[c]Literally, *is it a great thing.*   [d]Cf. v. 2.
[e]Literally, *we put up with all things.*
[f]Literally, *partake with the altar.*   [g]Cf. Luke 10:7.

¹⁹Although I am free from all men, I made myself a slave to all, in order that I might win as many as possible. ²⁰Thus to the Jews I became like a Jew, that I might win Jews. To men under the Law [I became] like one under the Law—although I am not under the Law myself—that I might win those under the Law. ²¹To men without [revealed] law [I became] like one without [revealed] law—although I am not outside God's law but inside the law of Christ—that I might win those who are without [revealed] law. ²²When dealing with oversensitive persons, I have looked at things from their viewpoint[h] that I might win them. I have become all things to all men, in order that by all means I might save some. ²³Everything I do is for the sake of the gospel, that I might share its blessing with others.[i]

²⁴You know, do you not, that all the competitors in a race try to win, but only one gets the prize? So you [in the life of faith] must run in such a way to win. ²⁵All those who strive to win in an athletic contest maintain self-control in every respect. They do so in order to receive a perishable crown,[j] but we [strive for] an imperishable one. ²⁶Accordingly, as I run I keep the goal clearly in view.[k] Like a boxer, I strike direct blows—I do not beat the air. ²⁷I practice severe self-discipline and keep my body under control, to make sure that after having preached to others, I myself may not fail to stand the test.

Chapter 10

Now I want you to remember, brothers, that our forefathers were all protected by the cloud,[a] and all passed through the sea,[b] ²and by the cloud [above them] and by the sea [on both sides of them][c] they were all submerged[d] in relation to Moses. ³They all ate the same supernatural food,[e] ⁴and all drank from the same supernatural stream,[f] for they were drinking from the supernatural Rock that accompanied them, and that Rock was Christ. ⁵Yet [in spite of their

---

hLiterally, *to the weak I became weak.* Cf. 8:7ff.
iOr, so that I might become a joint-partaker in it.
jOr, a wreath of fading leaves.   kOr, I run with no uncertainty.
aLiterally, *were all under the cloud.* Cf. Exod. 13:21-22.   bCf. Exod. 14:29.
cCf. Exod. 14:19-22; Ps. 105:39.   dOr, baptized.
eCf. Exod. 16:13-21; PS. 78:24-28.   fCf. Exod. 17:6; Num. 20:7-11; 21:16.

extraordinary privileges[g]] God was not pleased with most of them,[h] for they were overthrown in the desert.[i]

[6]Those events have become illustrations[j] for us, to warn us not to crave evil things as did our forefathers.[k] [7]Do not become idolaters as some of them did, for it stands written, "The people sat down to eat and drink, and rose up to dance in idol worship.[l] [8]Neither let us commit fornication as some of them did, and [as a result of their immorality] twenty-three thousand of them fell in one day.[m] [9]Nor let us provoke the Lord to such limits that his longsuffering ceases, as some did and [as a result] were killed by serpents.[n] [10]Neither complain, as some of them did and [consequently] perished at the hands of the Destroyer.[o]

[11]What happened to our forefathers are illustrations,[p] and were recorded to warn us who are living at the consummation of the ages. [12]Therefore let the man who thinks he is standing make sure that he does not fall. [13]No temptation has come upon you except that which is common to human nature. But God is faithful, and he will not permit you to be tempted beyond your strength. Along with the temptation he will make the way out, so that you can bear up under it.[q]

[14]Therefore, my beloved, always avoid idolatry. [15]I speak as to sensible men, so weigh carefully what I say. [16]Is not the consecrated cup, over which we pray, a means of communion in the blood of Christ? Is not the bread which we break a means of communion in the body of Christ? [17]Because there is one loaf of bread, we, who are many, constitute one body. For we all partake of the one loaf.

[18]Consider [the practice of] literal Isarel: Do not those who eat [their portion of] the sacrifices enter into communion with the altar? [19]Now what do I mean? [Do I infer] that an idolatrous sacrifice has any value, or that an idol actually exists? [20]No, but what [the heathen] sacrifice, they actually sacrifice to demons and not to God.[r]

---

[g]Very impressive is the five-fold use of the term *all* in the enumeration of the divine favors bestowed upon the entire company of Israelites (vv. 1-4).
[h]Cf. Num. 14:29-30.   [i]Or, [their corpses] were scattered over the wilderness.
[j]Greek, *tupoi*, types, patterns, or examples. Here in a sense not to be imitated.
[k]Literally, *as those indeed craved.*   [l]Cf. Exod. 32:6; Acts 7:41.
[m]Cf. Num. 25:9.   [n]Cf. Num. 21:5f.; Ps. 78:17ff.   [o]Cf. Num. 16:41ff.
[p]Literally, *these things happened typically to those men.*
[q]Or, the way out, which consists of the power to endure.
[r]Cf. Deut. 32:17; Ps. 106:37.

And I do not want you to have any communion with demons. [21]You cannot drink the cup of the Lord and the cup of demons. You cannot partake of the Lord's table and of the demons' table. [22]Are we provoking the Lord to anger [by trying to divide our devotion between him and demons]?[s]

[23]"All things are permissible," it is said.[t] But not all things are beneficial. "All things are permissible," some contend. But not all things build up character. [24]Let no one seek his own [well-being] but that of the other person. [25]Eat anything you buy in a public market, asking no questions [about its source or previous use]. [26]For "The earth is the Lord's, and so is everything that is in it."[u] [27]If someone who is not a believer invites you [to his house], and you go, eat whatever is placed before you, asking no questions on grounds of conscience. [28]But if you are told, "This food was used in idol worship,"[v] then out of consideration for your informant, and for conscience' sake, do not eat it. [29]I do not mean your conscience but the conscience of the oversensitive individual.

"But," [you may protest) "why should my freedom be restricted by another man's conscience? [30]If I partake with gratitude, and give thanks [for what I eat] why am I denounced?" [31]Because whether you eat or drink, or whatever you do, you are to do it all for God's glory.[32]So do not be a cause of stumbling either to Jews or to Greeks or to the church of God. [33]I, too, try to please all people in everything, not seeking my own well-being but that of the many in order that they may be saved.

Chapter 11

Follow my example, even as I also follow Christ's.[a] [2]Now I commend you for remembering me in all things, and for holding fast the

---

[s]Or, by putting him in the same category with demons? Cf. Deut. 32:21; Ezek. 20:39.
[t]Cf. 6:12.
[u]Cf. Ps. 24:1; 50:12.
[v]Literally, *This is temple meat. Hierothuton* means *a sacred sacrifice.* Such a statement would be made from the pagan viewpoint. A Jew or a Christian would ordinarily use the term *eidōlothuton, a thing sacrificed to an idol,* as in the variant reading here. Cf. 1 Cor. 8:7; 10:19; Acts 21:25. See the genitive plural *eidōlothutōn* in 1 Cor. 8:1, 4; Acts 15:29; and the accusative neuter plural *eidōlothuta* in 1 Cor. 8:10; Rev. 2:14, 20.
[a]This verse may well be part of Chapter 10.

doctrines[b] exactly as I delivered them to you. 3But I want you to realize that Christ is the head of every man, the husband is the head of the wife,[c] and God is the head of Christ. 4Any man who engages in [public] prayer or prophesying[d] with his head covered dishonors his head. 5But any woman who engages in [public] prayer or prophesying with her head uncovered dishonors her head, for she might just as well have her head shaved.[e]

6Indeed, if a woman does not wear a veil, let her also cut off her hair. But if it is shameful for a woman to cut off her hair or to shave her head, let her wear a veil. 7A man ought not to cover his head, for he is a visible representation of God.[f] But woman is man's counterpart.[g] 8Indeed, man was not [created] from woman, but woman [was created] from man.[h] 9Nor was man created for woman's sake, but woman [was created] for man's sake.[i]

10Therefore, a woman ought to cover her head as an acknowledgment of her divinely appointed status[j] because of the angels.[k] 11However, in the Lord the woman is not [complete] without the man, nor is the man [complete] without the woman. 12For just as the woman [was created] from the man,[l] so also man [comes into existence] by means of woman. And all things have their source in God.

13Decide for yourselves: Is it proper for a woman to engage in [public] prayer to God with her head uncovered? 14Does not nature itself teach you that if a man wears his hair long it is a disgrace to him? 15But that if a woman wears her hair long it is a thing of beauty to her?[m] Long hair has been given to her for a covering. 16But if anyone presumes to be contentious [about this matter], we have no such custom, nor [have] the churches of God.

17There is a matter about which I cannot commend you: Some of your meetings are not achieving their purpose—they result in more harm than good. 18In the first place, I keep hearing that when you come together as a church there are cliques among you, and I

---

[b]Greek, *paradoseis, things handed over, traditions.* Used here by Paul of truths to be handed down to believers. Cf. 2 Thess. 2:15; 3:6.
[c]Literally, *the man is the head of the woman.*
[d]Inspired preaching or teaching. Cf. 1 Cor. 14:3.
[e]Literally, *for it is one and the same thing as if she were shaved.*
[f]Literally, *he is God's image and glory.* Cf. Gen. 1:26, 27.
[g]Literally, *man's glory.*   [h]Cf. Gen. 2:23.
[i]Cf. Gen. 2:18.   [j]Or, ought to have [a symbol of] authority on her head.
[k]Cf. Gen. 2:18.   [l]Cf. Gen. 2:21-23.
[m]Literally, *it is a glory to her.*

believe some of these reports. [19]Of course differences of opinion among you are necessary in order that men of competence[n] may become known.

[20]But to resume my point, when you meet together you do not really observe the Lord's Supper. [21]For each one is in a hurry to eat his own supper, and some begin before the rest are ready, with the result that there are those who remain hungry while others drink to excess. [22]Surely you have homes of your own in which to eat, have you not? Or do you treat with contempt the church of God, and humiliate the poor? What shall I say? Can I commend you? No! For such conduct I cannot commend you!

[23]As a matter of fact I myself received from the Lord that which I handed on to you: The Lord Jesus in the night when he was being betrayed took bread [24]and, after giving thanks, he broke it and said, "This is my body which is for you. Do this from time to time[o] in remembrance of me." [25]In like manner also [he took] the cup, after the supper, saying, "This cup is the new covenant [validated] by my blood. Do this from time to time,[o] as often as you drink it, in remembrance of me." [26]For each time you eat this bread and drink the cup you proclaim the Lord's death until he comes.

[27]Consequently, whoever eats the bread or drinks the cup of the Lord in an unworthy manner will be guilty with regard to the body and the blood of the Lord. [28]But [in order to avoid such guilt] let a man [first] put himself to the test[p] and, after so doing, let him eat of the bread and drink of the cup. [29]For whoever eats and drinks without recognizing [the significance of] His body, eats and drinks judgment against himself.

[30]That is why many among you are weak and ill, and a considerable number are dying.[q] [31]But if we would make a practice of carefully examining ourselves, we would not be undergoing judgment. [32]Yet when we incur the Lord's judgment, we are being disciplined[r] in order that we may not be condemned along with the world.

---

[n]Literally, *those who stand the test.*
[o]Implied by *poieite*, present imperative.
[p]Or, test his spiritual condition.
[q]Literally, *are sleeping.* Sleep is a euphemism for death. Cf. 15:6, 18, 20, 51; 1 Thess. 4:13-15.
[r]Or, Yet when we are judged, we are being disciplined by the Lord.

³³So, my brothers, when you come together to eat, wait for one another. ³⁴If anyone attends merely to eat and drink,ˣ let him gratify his hunger at home, so that your meetings may not bring condemnation upon you. I will set the other matters in order when I come.

Chapter 12

Now concerning spiritual manifestations, brothers, I want you to be adequately informed. ²You recall that when you were pagans you used to be swept away, whenever the impulse happened to seize you,ᵃ to idols that could impart no knowledge. ³Let me give you the criteria for testing spiritual expression: No one speaking under the influence of the Spirit of God declares "Jesus be cursed!" And no one is able to say "Jesus is Lord!" except by the influence of the Holy Spirit.

⁴There are varieties of gifts, but they are from the same Spirit. ⁵And there are varieties of ministries, but it is the same Lord [who enables us to serve]. ⁶And there are varieties of activities, but it is the same God who energizes every person. ⁷To each one is given the manifestation of the Spirit with a view to the common good. ⁸To one is given, by the Spirit, discourse characterized by wisdom. To another, discourse characterized by knowledge according to the same Spirit. ⁹To another, [extraordinary] faithᵇ by the same Spirit. To another, gifts to heal different kinds of diseasesᶜ by the one Spirit. ¹⁰And to another, the working of miracles.ᵈ And to another, prophecy.ᵉ And to another, the ability to discriminate between true and false spirits.ᶠ To another, various languages. And to another, interpretation of languages. ¹¹But all these are imparted by the one and same Spirit, who distributes them to each individual exactly as He chooses.

¹²For just as the [natural] body is one and has many members, and all the members, though many, constitute one body, so it is with Christ [in whom all believers are one]. ¹³Indeed, by means of one Spirit all of us—whether Jews or Greeks, whether slaves or free men—

ˢOr, If anyone is too hungry to wait.
ᵃCf. 10:20.
ᵇCf. 13:2; Matt. 17:20; 21:21; Mark 11:22-24.   ᶜLiterally, *gifts of cures.*
ᵈLiterally, *operations of powers.*   ᵉOr, inspired preaching or teaching. Cf. 14:3.
ᶠLiterally, *discernings of spirits.* Cf. 1 John 4:1.

were baptized into one body, and all were given to drink of one Spirit. [14]So, the body does not consist of one member but of many.

[15]If the foot were to say, "Because I am not a hand, I am not part of the body," it would not cease being part of the body. [16]If the ear were to say, "Because I am not an eye, I am not part of the body," it would not cease being part of the body. [17]If the entire body were an eye, how could anyone hear? If the entire body were an ear, how could anyone smell? [18]But the fact is, God has placed the members—every one of them—in the body just as he wished.

[19]If the whole were just one part, how could there be a body? [20]Actually there are many members, but there is only one body. [21]The eye cannot say to the hand, "I do not need you;" nor can the head say to the feet, "I do not need you." [22]On the contrary,[g] the members of the body which seem to be weaker are certainly necessary, [23]and those parts which we regard as less honorable are the ones which we surround with more abundant honor.[h] And the least presentable parts are treated with special consideration [24]which our more presentable parts do not require.

But God has formed the body in such a way that special dignity has been given to the [seemingly] inferior parts, [25]in order that there may not be any discord in the body, but that the members should exercise mutual concern for one another. [26]So if one member suffers, all the members suffer with it; if one member is honored, all the members rejoice with it.

[27]Now you—the congregation—are a body in relation to Christ, and each member has his function to perform. [28]And God has placed in the church first, apostles; second, prophets; third, teachers; next, miraculous powers; then gifts of cures, abilities for rendering assistance, capacities for leadership, facility in various languages.

[29]All are not apostles, are they?[i] All are not prophets, are they? All are not teachers, are they? All are not workers of miracles, are they? [30]All do not have gifts of cures, do they? All do not speak in foreign languages, do they? All do not interpret, do they? [31] [j]Earnestly desire[k] the greater gifts, and yet I want to show you a way that far surpasses them.

---

[g]Literally, *But by much more.*　　[h]Or, which we clothe with special care.
[i]Every question in this and the following verse is introduced by the Greek negative particle *mē*, which indicates that in each instance the answer *No* is expected.
[j]This verse might well be placed with chapter 13.　　[k]Cf. v. 11.

Chapter 13

If I spoke with the eloquence of men and even of angels, but lacked love,[a] my oratory would amount to no more than unimpressive loquacity.[b] 2And if I had prophetic insight and knew all the secret truths and all the knowledge [available to man], and if I could exercise the widest range of faith—even to move mountains—but had not love, I would be nothing. 3And if I gave away all my possessions, and actually sacrificed my body to be burned, but had no love, it would profit me nothing.

4This love [to which I refer] is long-suffering and kind. It is not envious. It does not put itself on display. It is not arrogant. 5It does not express itself in a rude manner. It is not selfish. It is not irritable. It keeps no record of evil [done to it]. 6It does not rejoice over wrongdoing but it rejoices with the truth. 7It does not unnecessarily expose anyone.[c] It is eager to believe the best [about everybody]. It tries to find hope in every situation. It perseveres in all circumstances.

8Love will never lose its preeminence.[d] Where there are prophetic activities, they will be terminated. Where there is eloquent speech, it will cease. Where there is knowledge, it will be transcended. 9Indeed, our knowledge is only partial, and our prophesying[e] is partial. 10But when that which is perfect comes, all that is partial will be superseded.

11When I was a child, I used to talk like a child, I used to think like a child, I used to make plans like a child; but now that I have become a man, I have given up permanently the ways of a child. 12Actually, at the present we see only dim reflections as if we were looking in a mirror, but then [we shall see] face to face. Now I know in part, but then I shall know as fully as I myself am known. 13And so faith, hope, and love remain—these three—but the greatest of these is love.

---

aThe Greek word for *love* used throughout this chapter is *agapē*, which denotes God's love made known in Christ and shed forth into the believer's heart by the Holy Spirit (cf. Rom. 5:5).

bLiterally, *I have become a noisy gong or a rattling cymbal.*

cLiterally, *It puts a roof over everything.*

dLiterally, *Love never fails.*

eOr, preaching.

Chapter 14

Keep pursuing divine love[a] [as your foremost aim because it is indispensable], yet continue to be zealous for spiritual endowments, especially for the gift of persuasive preaching.[b] [2]He who speaks in a foreign language[c] speaks not to men but to God, for no one[d] understands him. But by the Spirit[e] he declares revealed truths.[f] [3]However, the one who preaches persuasively addresses men [in a way that brings] edification and admonition and consolation. [4]He who speaks in a foreign language edifies himself, but the persuasive preacher builds up [the spiritual life of] the church. [5]Now I might wish[g] that all of you could speak in foreign languages. But I much prefer you to be persuasive preachers.[h] He who preaches persuasively renders a more useful service than he who speaks in foreign languages—unless, of course, the latter interprets [what he says], so that the church may receive benefit.[i]

[6]Now, brothers, if I come to you and speak in foreign languages, what good can I do you unless my words convey some meaning either by revelation, or by knowledge, or by clear preaching, or by teaching? [7]It is the same with inanimate things, [j] such as the flute or the harp —if they do not make a distinction in the notes, how can the melody

---

[a]Greek, *agapē*.   [b]Literally, *but rather that you may prophesy.*

[c]Corinth was a flourishing commercial city, with harbors on two seas. Its population came from all parts of the known world, hence the members of the church there would reflect many languages and dialects.

[d]"No one" is not to be taken in the absolute sense. The speaker would understand and give the interpretation (cf. vv. 5, 6, 13-17), or someone else conversant with the particular language could do so (cf. vv. 27-28; 12:30). The whole context indicates that anything spoken under the impetus of the Holy Spirit is intelligible. A difficulty might arise because of the languages used, but not because of the absence of meaning.

[e]Cf. 2:13; Acts 2:4.   [f]Literally, *mysteries.*

[g]Or, I wish. The Greek verb, *thelō* is the form of both the subjunctive and the indicative. In the present context it seems to be the subjunctive, i.e., it expresses a hypothetical statement.

[h]Reiteration of preference stated in v. 1.

[i]Paul is dealing with young converts, many of whom were former pagans. Some faults of their pre-Christian experience were re-appearing or, more probably, had not yet been overcome. The Corinthians needed to understand the nature of spiritual gifts, and to escape the perils of false expressions. Pagan worship was characterized by frenzied, ecstatic utterances over which reason had no control. Paul does not approve unreasoning emotionalism. His purpose is to lead the Christian believers completely away from the old cultic behavior patterns. To this end he writes in a diplomatic manner and takes a positive approach, emphasizing the qualities and procedures which are paramount in the new life.

[j]Literally, *with lifeless things giving a sound.*

be recognized?[k] [8]Again, if a military trumpet does not sound a clear signal, who will prepare himself for battle? [9]So it is with you—unless you speak clearly, how will anyone know what you say? Actually, you will be speaking into the air.

[10]There are, we may say, many different kinds of speech in the world, and none is without meaning. [11]If, however, I do not know the significance of the language [being spoken], I am a stranger to the speaker and the speaker is a stranger to me. [12]So with you, since you are eager for spiritual manifestations, strive especially for excellence in edifying the church.

[13]This is why anyone who speaks in a foreign language should pray that he may interpret [what he says to his hearers]. [14]If I pray[l] in a foreign language, my spirit prays but my understanding produces no fruit [for the benefit of others]. [15]What is the inference of what I have been saying? I will pray with the spirit but I will also pray so as to be understood[m] [by my listeners]. I will sing with the spirit but I will also sing so as to be understood[m] [by my listeners[n]].

[16]Otherwise suppose you are giving thanks [to God] in spirit [only], how can the person who is not conversant [with the language you use] say Amen to your thanksgiving if he does not understand what you are talking about? [17]Indeed you give thanks in a manner edifying to yourself,[o] but the other person receives no benefit [unless he understands what you say]. [18]I thank God that I might speak[p] in foreign languages more than all of you. [19]Nevertheless, in church I would rather speak five words which are understood,[q] in order that I might instruct others,[r] than [to speak] ten thousand words in a foreign language.

[20]Brothers, do not be children in your thinking. Be babes where malice is concerned, but in your thinking be mature. [21]In the Law[x]

---

[k]Literally, *how can what is played on the flute or on the harp be known?*

[l]A third class condition. It expresses a hypothetical statement, not a declaration of fact.   [m] Literally, *with the understanding also.*   [n]Indicated by vv. 16-19.

[o]Literally, *you yourself give thanks well.* This implies that the speaker is benefited, hence understands what he says. Paul nowhere sanctions meaningless utterance.

[p]Or, I speak. The Greek verb *lalō* is the form of the indicative as well as the form of the subjunctive. In this context (note especially v. 19) it seems to be subjunctive. Cf. same idiom with *thelō* in v. 5. Paul was a versatile linguist. From his cultural background and schooling he learned Hebrew, Aramaic, Greek, and, probably, Latin. As the Apostle to the Gentiles his evangelistic tours carried him into provinces where many local dialects were spoken.   [q]Literally, *five words with my understanding.*

[r]Thus Paul explains what he means by speaking with the understanding.

[x]Here *the Law* refers to the Old Testament Scriptures as a whole. Cf. John 10:34; 12:34; 15:25; Rom. 3:19.

it stands written, "By men of foreign languages and through the lips of strangers I will speak to this people, and not even then will they listen to me, says the Lord."[t] [22]This shows that foreign languages are a sign[u] not to those who believe but to those who do not believe, whereas the clear presentation of God's word[v] is intended not for unbelievers but for believers.

[23]Consequently, if the entire church meets together in one place, and all speak in foreign languages, and uninformed persons or unbelievers come in, will they not say you are crazy? [24]But if everyone proclaims God's word clearly,[w] and some unbeliever or uninformed person comes in, he is convicted by all, he is searched out by all, [25]he sees himself as he is.[x] And so he will bow down and worship God, confessing, "Truly God is among you!"

[26]What are the implications of what I have been saying, brothers?[y] When you meet together, each one has [a contribution to make]: a hymn, a teaching, a revelation, a discourse in a foreign language, or an interpretation. Let all things be done with a view to [the] upbuilding [of the church]. [27]If any speak in a foreign language, let only two or at the most three, speak, one at a time, and let someone interpret what is said.

[28]However if no interpreter is present,[z] let the one who would speak in a foreign language keep silent in the church, and let him speak to himself and to God. [29]Let two or three prophets speak, and

[t]Cf. Isa. 28:11-12. Israel heard God's word, delivered plainly by the prophets, but refused to obey. As a result, divine judgment is pronounced upon the rebellious people and God says they will be conquered by barbarous strangers whose language they cannot understand. The prediction was fulfilled by the Assyrian invasion (cf. 2 Chron. 28:16ff.). That historical incident is analogous to the situation to which Paul applies it. He points out that just as words spoken in strange speech did not lead the Hebrews to obedience, so speaking in foreign languages will not profit the Corinthians.

[u]Not a convincing sign, but one which does not favorably impress unbelievers (cf. v. 23). For other instances of *sēmeion* as a *sign* with a negative effect, cf. Luke 2:34; John 2:18; Matt. 12:39; 16:4.

[v]Literally, *prophecy.*

[w]Literally, *But if all prophesy.* Expression in foreign languages has value only through the aid of another gift, i.e., interpretation, whereas persuasive preaching is of first importance because unaided it sets forth the gospel.

[x]Literally, *the secrets of his heart are exposed.* Cf. Heb. 4:12-13.

[y]Literally, *What therefore is it, brothers?*

[z]This implies that a person needing an interpreter is able to ascertain in advance whether or not an interpreter is present. This could not be done if nonhuman or heavenly languages were involved; for if that were the case the interpretation would have to come as a special disclosure in each instance, hence a speaker could never be certain that he should present a message.

let the others consider carefully what is said. [30]And if anything is revealed to another who is sitting by, let the first speaker yield to him. [31]For you can all declare God's message[a] one by one, so that all may learn and be encouraged.

[32]The spirits of inspired men are under the control of the inspired men[b] [33]For God is not [the Author] of disorder but of peace, as [he is] in all the churches of the saints.[c]

[34]Let the women maintain silence in the churches. They are not permitted to disturb the decorum of worship,[d] but are to be submissive even as also the Law says.[e] [35]And if they wish to learn about something, let them ask their own husbands at home. For it is a shame for a woman to disturb the decorum of worship. [36]Was it with you that the word of God originated? Or are you the only people it has reached?

[37]If anyone claims to be a prophet or to have any spiritual endowment, let him acknowledge that what I am writing to you is a command of the Lord. [38]But if anyone disregards this, he should be disregarded.

[39]So then, my brothers, be eager to preach persuasively,[f] and do not forbid anyone who has the gift of speaking in foreign languages to exercise it. [40]But let everything be done in a proper and orderly manner.

Chapter 15

Now I want to remind you, brothers, of the gospel which I preached to you, and which you received, and in which you are

---

[a]Literally, *prophesy.*

[b]That is, their emotions and speech are governed by their understanding and their will. The violent possession which often seized heathen spokesmen and overpowered their reason and self-consciousness is foreign to the motivation of the Holy Spirit.

[c]This last clause may be connected with vs. 34. The thought would then be. As in all the churches of the saints, let the women maintain silence in the meetings.

[d]Literally, *they are not permitted to continue speaking; i.e.,* whispering and asking their husbands questions during church services. This interpretation is suggested by the present infinitive of the onomatopoetic verb *laleō,* and by the permissive arm of the antithesis contained in v. 35.

[e]No such prohibition is found in the Mosaic Law, hence *the Law* here refers to the Old Testament in general (as in v. 21) which subordinates woman to man in the account of creation (Gen. 2:21-23), and by the primeval pronouncement given in Genesis 3:16.   [f]Or, to prophesy.

standing firm, [2]and through which you are being saved, if you are holding fast the word exactly as I proclaimed it to you, unless you have no real basis for your faith.[a] [3]For, I handed on to you matters of first importance, which also I received: that Christ died for our sins, as the Scriptures had foretold. [4]That he was buried, and that on the third day he was raised[b] from the dead, as the Scriptures foretold, [5]and that he was seen by Cephas, and then by the Twelve.

[6]After that, he was seen on one occasion by more than five hundred brothers, most of whom are still alive, although some of them have fallen asleep. [7]Next he was seen by James, then by all the apostles. [8]And finally he was seen by me, as by one born out of due time.[c]

[9]For I myself am the least of the apostles—in fact, I am not fit to be called an apostle, because I persecuted the church of God. [10]But by God's grace I am what I am. And his favor toward me was not wasted. Actually, I toiled more abundantly than any of the others. Yet it was not I, but the grace of God which is with me. [11]But whether it was I or they, this is what we preach, and this is what you came to believe.

[12]Now if we preach that Christ has been raised from the dead, how can some among you say there is no [such thing as a] resurrection of the dead? [13]If there is no resurrection of the dead, neither has Christ been raised. [14]And if Christ has not been raised, then our proclamation is empty and your faith is in vain. [15]Furthermore, we are found guilty of misrepresenting God because we testified that he raised up Christ—which is not true if indeed the dead are not to be raised. [16]For if the dead are not to be raised, neither has Christ been raised. [17]And if Christ has not been raised, your faith is futile— you are yet in your sins. [18]Also it follows that those who have fallen asleep [trusting] in Christ have perished. [19]If our hope in Christ does not extend beyond this life, we of all people are to be most pitied.

[20]But the fact is, Christ has been raised from the dead [and continues to live in his risen state[d]] and he is the Prototype[e] of those who

---

[a]Literally, *unless indeed you believed in vain.*

[b]The perfect passive indicative, *egēgertai*, means *he was raised up, and continues to live as risen.* Thus are emphasized the fact of the resurrection of Christ and the permanent results of the event.   [c]Literally, *like an abortion.*

[d]See note on 15:4.

[e]Greek, *aparchē, firstfruits.* As the wave sheaf (Lev. 23:10) was the pattern viewed in anticipation of the complete harvest, so Christ is the Firstfruits and pledge of the general resurrection which is to take place at the close of the age (cf. Matt. 13:39).

have fallen asleep. 21For since through a man came death, also through a Man comes the resurrection of the dead. 22As in connection with Adam, all men die, so also in connection with Christ all shall be made alive. 23But each in his proper order: Christ the Prototype, and afterwards, at Christ's appearance, those who belong to him. 24Then comes the consummation when, after subduing completely all rule and every authority and power, he delivers the kingdom to God the Father. 25For he must reign until he has put all his enemies under his feet.*f* 26The last enemy to be destroyed is death. Indeed, God has placed all things under Christ's feet. 27But when the Scripture declares that all things have been put in subjection, it is obvious that the One who put them in subjection is excepted. 28But when all things have been subjected to him, then the Son himself will also be subjected to the One who put all things under him, so that God may be all in all.*g*

29If there is no resurrection,*h* what shall those achieve who are being baptized because of*i* [the influence of] the dead? If the dead are not raised at all, why indeed are [some people] being baptized out of respect for them? 30And why do we ourselves face danger every moment? 31I am proud of what Christ Jesus our Lord has wrought in you, brothers, and so I am [willing to be] exposed to death from day to day.

32If from a mere temporal point of view I fought with beasts at Ephesus, what did I gain? If the dead are never raised [we might as well say with others], "Let us eat and drink, for tomorrow we die!"*j* 33Stop being led astray. Bad company corrupts good morals. 34Return at once to your right senses, and avoid sinning. Actually, some individuals have no knowledge of God. I say this to make you feel ashamed.

35But someone will ask, How are the dead raised? What kind of body will they have? 36Think about some analogies from nature.*k* The seed you yourself sow does not come to life unless it dies. 37And what you plant is not the form that is to be, but it is a bare seed, perhaps a grain of wheat or something else. 38But God gives it a form in accordance with his will—to each kind of seed a form of its own.

---

*f*Cf. Pss. 8:6; 110:1.
*h*Literally, *Otherwise.*
*j*Cf. Isa. 22:13.

*g*Or, so that God may be everything to everyone.
*i*Rendering the preposition *huper* as causal.
*k*Literally, *You unthinking man!*

[39]Not all flesh is the same: human beings have one kind of flesh, beasts another, birds another, and fish another. [40]And there are bodies which are adapted to a heavenly existence, and there are bodies which are adapted to an earthly existence. But the splendor of the heavenly is different from the splendor of the earthly. [41]There is a splendor of the sun, and another splendor of the moon, and another splendor of the stars. And star differs from star in splendor.

[42]So it is with the resurrection of the dead. The body is sown in corruption; it is raised in incorruptibility. [43]It is sown in dishonor; it is raised in glory. It is sown in weakness; it is raised in power. [44]It is sown a natural body; it is raised a spiritual body. As surely as there is a natural body, there is also a spiritual body.

[45]Thus it stands written, "Adam, the first man, became a living being."[l] The last Adam is a life-giving Spirit. [46]Yet it is not the spiritual which comes first, but the natural. Afterwards comes the spiritual. [47]The first man is of the earth—earthly by nature. The Second Man is from heaven. [48]Those who are earthly are like him who was of the earth, and those who are heavenly are like Him who is from heaven. [49]And just as we did reflect the likeness of the earthly man, let us also reflect[m] the likeness of the Heavenly Man. [50]What I mean, brothers, is that nothing of the character of flesh and blood can inherit the kingdom of God, nor can corruption inherit incorruptibility.

[51]Behold, I declare to you a revealed secret: We shall not all fall asleep, but we shall all be changed, [52]in an instant,[n] as quickly as the glance of an eye, when the last trumpet sounds. For the trumpet will sound, and the dead will be raised free from corruption—never to experience death again—and we shall be changed.

[53]For this corruptible nature must put on incorruptibility, and this mortal nature must put on immortality. [54]And when this corruptible nature puts on incorruptibility, and this mortal nature puts on immortality, then shall come to pass the saying that stands written, "Death has been completely overcome by victory."[o] [55]"Where, O

---

[l]Cf. Gen. 2:7.

[m]Rendering *phoresōmen,* aorist subjunctive. Some manuscripts read *phoresomen,* future indicative, *we shall reflect.*

[n]The Greek word, *atomos,* means that which cannot be cut or divided (our word *atom*). Here it signifies the suddenness of the transformation, which will take place in the smallest possible unit of time.

[o]Cf. Isa. 25:8.

Death, is your victory? Where, O Death, is your sting?"[p] [56]Now the sting of death is sin, and the power of sin is the Law.[q] [57]But thanks be to God who gives us the victory through our Lord Jesus Christ!

[58]Therefore, my beloved brothers, prove yourselves stedfast, unmovable, always abounding in the Lord's work, because you know that your labor in [the service of] the Lord is never in vain.

Chapter 16

Now concerning the collection to aid the saints,[a] you should follow the same procedure I designated for the churches of Galatia.[b] [2]On the first day of every week, let each of you put aside something, in proportion to what he earns, and store it up so that no special appeals will need to be made when I come. [3]After my arrival, I will give letters of introduction to men approved by you, and send them to carry your gift to Jerusalem. [4]If the contribution is large enough to make it expedient for me to go too,[c] your representatives[d] can make the journey with me.

[5]I shall come to you after I have visited the Macedonian churches.[e] I do plan to travel through Macedonia, [6]and possibly I shall spend some time with you—perhaps the whole winter,[f] after which[g] you can send me on toward my next destination.[h] [7]I do not want to pay you a mere passing visit now. Instead, I hope to stay with you for some length of time, if the Lord permits. [8]However, my present plans are to remain in Ephesus until Pentecost, [9]for a great door of opportunity stands wide open for me [here], and there are many persons who would like to shut it.[i]

[10]When Timothy[j] arrives, make him feel at ease among you, for he is engaged in the Lord's work just as I am. [11]So let no one treat him with disrespect, but send him on his way in peace so that he may return to me. For I am expecting him with the brothers.

---

[p]Cf. Hos. 13:14.   [q]Cf. Rom. 7:5-20.

[a]That is, for the needy people of God in Judea. Cf. Acts 11:29-30; 24:17; Rom. 15:25ff.; 2 Cor. 8:4; 9:1, 12.   [b]Cf. Acts 18:23.

[c]Literally, *And if it is fitting that I should go also.*   [d]Literally, *they.*

[e]Literally, *after I have gone through Macedonia.* Cf. Acts 20:1-2.   [f]Cf. Acts 20:3.

[g]Literally, *in order that.*   [h]Literally, *wherever I may go.*

[i]Literally, *and there are many adversaries.*

[j]Cf. Acts 19:22; 1 Cor. 4:17.

¹²Concerning our brother Apollos, I strongly urged him to accompany the brothers for a visit with you, but it was not at all [his] will to come now. However, he will come when he has a good opportunity.

¹³Be alert at all times. Keep standing firm in the faith. Act like men. Grow in strength! ¹⁴Let all your actions be characterized by purposive good will.[k]

¹⁵You know that the family of Stephanas[l] were my first converts in Achaia, and that they have set themselves for service to the saints.

¹⁶I urge you, my brothers, to submit yourselves to such persons, and to everyone who is a fellow worker and laborer. ¹⁷I rejoice at the arrival of Stephanas and Fortunatus and Achaicus, because they have made up for the lack of your presence. ¹⁸They have refreshed my spirit, just as they did yours. So you should hold such men in high esteem.

¹⁹The churches [in the province] of Asia send you greetings. Aquila and Prisca, along with the church that meets in their house, greet you cordially in the Lord. ²⁰All the brothers send greetings to you. Greet one another with a holy kiss.

²¹This is my salutation, written with my own hand—Paul. ²²If anyone has no affection for the Lord, let him be anathema. Our Lord, come![m] ²³May the gracious favor of the Lord Jesus be with you. ²⁴My love be with you all in Christ Jesus.

---

[k]Literally, *Let everything of yours be done in love (agape).*   [l]Cf. 1:16.
[m]Rendering the Aramaic formula as imperative, *marana-tha.* The expression may be indicative, *maran-atha, Our Lord comes!*

SECOND CORINTHIANS

Chapter 1

Paul, an apostle of Christ Jesus by the will of God, and Timothy our brother, to the church of God which is at Corinth, and to all the saints in the whole [province] of Achaia:[a] [2]May gracious favor be yours, and peace from God our Father and the Lord Jesus Christ.

[3]Blessed be the God and Father of our Lord Jesus Christ, the Father of mercies and the God of all encouragement. [4]He consoles us in all our trouble so that, by the consolation which we ourselves receive from God, we may be able to console others who are in any trouble. [5]For as the sufferings of Christ overflow upon us, so also through Christ our consolation overflows. [6]If we endure trouble, it is for your encouragement and salvation. If we are consoled, it is for your consolation which shows its effectiveness in your endurance of the same sufferings which we ourselves undergo. [7]Our hope for you is well founded, because we know that as you share our sufferings, you will also share our comfort.

[8]Indeed we want you to know, brothers, that the trouble which we experienced in the [province of] Asia[b] was so utterly crushing that we despaired even of life. [9]Actually, in our hearts we felt the sentence of death. We realized that we could not depend upon ourselves[c] but upon God who raises the dead. [10]He rescued us out of imminent death, and he will do so again. And in him we maintain hope that he will deliver us in the future, [11]while you help us by prayer in our behalf, so that many persons may offer thanks for the blessing[d] granted to us through their intercession.

---

[a]Achaia included all of Greece south of Macedonia. Corinth was its capital, and there the proconsul resided (Acts 18:12). Athens, where there were believers, was in Achaia (cf. 17:34). There was a church in Cenchreae, the eastern seaport of Corinth (cf. Acts 18:18; Rom. 16:1). [b]Cf. Acts 19:23-41.

[c]Literally, *so that we might not rely upon ourselves.*

[d]Or, favor. Greek, *charisma,* gracious gift.

12We rejoice because our conscience tells us that we have conducted ourselves before the world and especially toward you in holiness and godly sincerity, not by human wisdom, but by God's grace. 13Indeed, we write to you only what you can read and understand, and I hope you will understand fully,*c* 14as also you understood in part, that on the Day of our Lord Jesus you may be as proud of us as we are of you.

15With this confidence [of mutual trust] I first intended to come to you before [going through Macedonia] in order that you might have the benefit of two visits from me. 16I planned to stop with you on my way to Macedonia, and again on my return from Macedonia, and then to be sent forward by you on my journey to Judea. 17Now in deciding on this I was not using fickleness, was I? Or did I make a decision like a worldly man, saying yes and no at the same time? 18As surely as God is reliable, our word to you is not yes and no.

19In fact God's Son, Christ Jesus—who was preached among you by us, by Silvanus and Timothy and myself—did not waver between yes and no, but in him we have the revelation of certainty.*f* 20For all the promises of God find their fulfillment in him.*g* That is why it is through him we say Amen when we give praise to God. 21And it is God who establishes us, along with you, in Christ. God has anointed us, 22and set his seal of ownership upon us, and given us the Spirit in our hearts, as a pledge of what is yet to come.

23Now upon my soul I call God as witness that the reason I did not come again to Corinth was to keep from embarrassing you. 24We have no desire to domineer over your faith. Rather we are contributors to your joy. As far as your faith is concerned, you are standing firm.

Chapter 2

I have resolved in my own mind not to make another painful visit to you. 2For if I cause you grief, who is there to make me glad except those who are being grieved by me? 3And I wrote about this change

---

*c*Or, acknowledge it until the end.
*f*Literally, *but in him has become yes.*
*g*Literally, *For however many are the promises of God, in him is the yes.*

of plan[a] so that when I do come back I shall not be grieved by those who ought to cause me to rejoice. I am convinced that what makes me glad will make all of you glad too. [4]I wrote to you out of much concern and anguish of heart, with many tears, not that you might be grieved but that you might be assured of the sacrificial love[b] which I have so abundantly for you.

[5]But if anyone has caused grief, it is not to me [only], but in some measure—not to speak too severely—to you all. [6]For the offender,[c] the censure by the majority of you is sufficient [punishment]. [7]You now must take the opposite course and forgive and comfort him, or he may be overwhelmed by excessive remorse. [8]So I exhort you to give him definite assurance of your love. [9]That is why I wrote, to test you, and find out whether you were obedient in every respect.

[10]When you forgive anyone, so do I. Indeed, what I have forgiven, if there has been anything to forgive, I have forgiven in the presence of Christ for your sake, [11]to prevent Satan from gaining an advantage over us. For we are aware of his schemes.

[12]When I arrived at Troas[d] to preach the gospel of Christ, I found a door of opportunity standing wide open for me in the Lord. [13]However, I was uneasy because Titus my brother did not meet me [with news about you]. So I took leave of the disciples there,[e] and went on to Macedonia.

[14]But thanks be to God who, in Christ, always leads us in triumph,[f] and wherever we go he uses us to spread the fragrance of the knowledge about himself. [15]For we are Christ's incense offered to God, manifested among those who are being saved and among those who are perishing. [16]To the latter it is an aroma which issues in death, and to the former an aroma which issues in life. And who is competent for this task? [17]Unlike so many who make merchandise of the word of God, we are men of sincerity, sent from God, and before God we speak in Christ.

---

aLiterally, *And I wrote this very thing.*
bGreek, *agapē.*
cLiterally, *For such a one.*
dOr, to the district around Troas.
eLiterally, *having taken leave of them.* Cf. Acts 20:6-7.
fOr, who always causes us to triumph.

Chapter 3

Are we beginning to commend ourselves again? Do we, as do certain persons, need letters of recommendation to you or from you? [2]You yourselves are our credentials,[a] written on our hearts, recognized and read by everyone.[b] [3]It is evident that you are a letter from Christ, composed as a result of our ministry—a letter inscribed not with ink but by the Spirit of the living God, not on stone slabs but on human hearts.

[4]Such is the confidence we have through Christ in our relation to God. [5]It is not that we consider ourselves to be adequate. We have no resources in ourselves, but our sufficiency comes from God. [6]It is he who has made us competent ministers of the new covenant—not [a covenant] of mere literal precepts but of the Spirit. Indeed, the written code kills [by bringing awareness of guilt[c]], but the Spirit imparts life.

[7]If the ministration characterized by death—[the Law of which was embodied] in letters engraved on stone[d]—was inaugurated with such splendor that the Israelites were not able to gaze intently upon Moses' face because of its brightness,[e] although that brightness was transitory,[f] [8]will not the ministration of the Spirit be more glorious? [9]For if the ministration characterized by death was glorious, the ministration characterized by righteousness is far more glorious. [10]Actually [the old system], glorious as it was, hardly seems glorious at all in comparison with the surpassing glory [of the new order]. [11]For if that which was transitory was glorious, that which is permanent is far more glorious.

[12]Because we have such a hope we speak with great openness— [13]unlike Moses, who used to cover his face with a veil to prevent the Israelites from looking at the end of what was being abolished. [14]Their senses were dulled; and to this day, when the old covenant is read, the same veil remains unlifted, for only through Christ is it removed. [15]Even to this very day, whenever Moses is read, a veil lies over their understanding. [16]But when a person turns to the Lord, that veil is stripped away. [17]Now the Lord is the Spirit,[g] and where the Spirit

[a]Or, letter of recommendation.
[b]Cf. 1 Cor. 1:4-6.   [c]Cf. Rom. 7:7-13.
[d]The Mosaic legislation was summed up in the Decalogue. Cf. Exod. 31:18.
[e]Cf. Exod. 34:29-35.   [f]Heb. 10:1ff.   [g]Cf. vv. 3, 6, 8.

of the Lord abides, there is freedom. ¹⁸And we all, from whose faces the veil has been lifted, reflect the splendor of the Lord, and we are being changed more and more into his likeness, by the influence of the Lord, the Spirit.

Chapter 4

Therefore, since it is by [God's] mercy that we are engaged in this ministry, we do not lose heart. ²We have renounced the hidden things of shame. We do not practice deceit, nor falsify the word of God. But by the clear presentation of the truth we commend ourselves to every man's conscience in the sight of God. ³If the gospel we preach is obscured, it is obscured to those who are perishing. ⁴The god of this age has blinded the perception of the unbelievers to prevent the light which proceeds from the gospel of the glory of Christ, who is the likeness of God, from dawning upon them.

⁵Certainly it is not ourselves that we preach. We preach Christ Jesus as Lord, and ourselves as your servants for Jesus' sake. ⁶Indeed, the same God who said, "Out of darkness light shall shine,"[a] is he who has shone in our hearts to enlighten us with the knowledge of God's glory [which is seen] in the face of Christ.

⁷But we have this treasure in frail bodies made of clay to show that its remarkable power comes from God and not from us. ⁸We are hard pressed from every direction, but not crushed; perplexed, but not to the point of despair; ⁹persecuted, but not abandoned [to the foe]; struck down, but not destroyed. ¹⁰At all times we are in danger of being put to death as Jesus was,[b] so that his life also may be manifested in our bodies. ¹¹That is to say, we the living are constantly being stalked by death for Jesus' sake, so that the life of Jesus may also be openly displayed in our mortal nature. ¹²So death is at work in us, but life is at work in you.

¹³Yet because we have the same spirit of faith which has been expressed in the words, "I believed, therefore I spoke,"[c] we too believe and so we speak. ¹⁴For we know that he who raised the Lord Jesus [from death] will also raise us with Jesus and will bring us,

[a]Cf. Gen. 1:3.

[b]Literally, *we always carry about in our bodies the dying of Jesus.* Cf. v. 11; 11:23; Phil. 3:10; 1 Cor. 15:31; Rom. 8:36; Gal. 6:17.   [c]Cf. Ps. 116:10.

along with you, [into his presence]. 15All these things are for your benefit, so that, as God's grace*d* reaches more and more people, the thanksgiving [which it induces] may abound to the glory of God.

16Therefore we do not lose heart. Although our outward nature is wearing away, nevertheless our inward nature is being renewed day by day. 17Of course we have trials, but actually they are light and momentary, and they are working out for us an eternal weight of glory which is incalculable. 18So we do not keep our attention on what is seen but on what is not seen. For the things that are seen are temporary, but the things that are not seen are eternal.

Chapter 5

For we know that if the present earthly dwelling in which we live is folded up like a tent, we have from God a building, a house not made by hands, that will last forever in heaven. 2Indeed, while we are in our present dwelling we yearn, eagerly longing to put on the habitation which is from heaven. 3For when we are clothed by it, we shall not be found without a body.

4In fact, while we are in this present earthly house, we keep yearning, being burdened not because we wish to put off [our earthly body] but to put on [our ultimate body], so that what is mortal may be superseded by life. 5It is God who has prepared us for this destiny,*a* and he has given us the Spirit as a pledge [that all his promises will be fulfilled].

6Therefore we are always confident, although we know that while our home is in the [present] body we are absent from [our home with] the Lord—7for we walk by faith, not by what is seen—8and in this confidence we would actually prefer to leave our home in the [present] body and to be at home with the Lord. 9So whether we are in our home or absent from it, our highest aim is to be well pleasing to him. 10For we must all be made manifest in our true character before the award-throne*b* of Christ, in order that each person may face what he did through the instrumentality of his body, and carry away with him the consequences of his deeds, whether excellent or worthless.

---

*d*Literally, *the grace.*   *a*Literally, *for this very thing.*   *b*Or, tribunal, or judgment-seat.

[11]Because we know what it means to fear the Lord, we are constantly trying to persuade men. Our motives have long been open before God, and I hope they are plain to your consciences. [12]We are not commending ourselves to you again, but giving you an incentive to be proud of us, so that you may have [an answer] for those who pride themselves on outward appearances and not on inward realities. [13]If we were ever beside ourselves, it was for God. If we are of sound mind, it is for you. [14]Indeed, the love exhibited by Christ possesses and motivates us. For we have concluded that One died for all, therefore all died. [15]And he died in behalf of all, in order that those who live should no longer live for themselves but for him who died for them and was raised [from death].

[16]From now on we regard no one according to outward appearance. Even though there was a time when we placed emphasis upon the outward appearance of Christ, we no longer regard him in that way. [17]So if anyone is in Christ, he is a new creation: the old relationships have passed away; behold, a new state of things has come. [18]And all this is the work of God, who through Christ reconciled us to himself, and gave us the ministry of reconciliation—[19]which is to say that God was in Christ reconciling the world to himself, not charging to men their misdeeds. And he has entrusted to us the message about this reconciliation. [20]Accordingly we are ambassadors on Christ's behalf, as if God were making his appeal through us. On behalf of Christ we plead, Get reconciled at once to God. [21]Although Christ never experienced any sin whatsoever, in our behalf God identified him with everything in the whole realm of sin in order that by trusting in him we might become [recipients of] God's kind of righteousness.

Chapter 6

As his fellow workers, we exhort you not to allow God's grace which you have received to become ineffective. [2]For he says, "In an acceptable time I listened to you, and in a day of deliverance I came to your aid."[a] Behold, now is the highly acceptable time! Behold, now is the day of salvation! [3]We put no hindrance in anyone's way, for we want to make sure that the ministry is not blamed.

[a]Cf. Isa. 49:8.

[4]Our lives reflect the marks of God's servants in every way: in great endurance, in oppressions, in calamities, in difficulties, [5]in floggings, in imprisonments, in [the midst of] riots, in arduous labor, in sleeplessness, in times without food; [6]by purity, by knowledge, by patience, by kindness, by the Holy Spirit,[b] by sincere love, [7]by truthful speech,[c] by the power of God. Equipped with the weapons supplied by righteousness for both offensive and defensive warfare.[d] [8]Through glory and dishonor, through blame and praise. Regarded as deceivers, although we are genuine. [9]Ignored, although we are well known. Constantly exposed to death, yet, behold, we go on living. Chastised, but not put to death. [10]Grieved, yet always rejoicing. Poor, but making many rich. Having nothing, yet possessing all things.

[11]We have spoken frankly to you, Corinthians. We have laid bare our heart, and it stands wide open [to receive you with love]. [12]If there is any restraint between us, it is not due to our lack of affection for you, but to your lack of affection for us. [13]Now to reciprocate in kind—I speak as to children—open wide your hearts to us.

[14]Do not become unequally yoked with unbelievers. For what do righteousness and lawlessness have in common? Or can light and darkness coexist? [15]Or what agreement is there between Christ and Beliar? Or what fellowship has a believer with a disbeliever? [16]Or what accord has God's sanctuary with idols? Indeed, we are a sanctuary of the living God, just as God said, "I will dwell in them, and walk among them. And I will be their God, and they shall be my people."[e] [17]Therefore, " 'Come out from their midst and be separate,' says the Lord, 'And avoid whatever is unclean.'[f] 'Then I will receive you, [18]and I will be your Father, and you shall be my sons and daughters,' says the Lord Almighty."[g]

Chapter 7

Since we are the recipients of these promises, beloved, let us cleanse ourselves from every defilement of body and of spirit, advancing toward the goal of complete holiness in the fear of God.

---

[b]Or, by holiness of spirit.   [c]Or, by the word of truth.
[d]Literally, for the right [hand] and the left.
[e]Cf. Lev. 26:11-12; Ezek. 37:27.   [f]Cf. Isa. 52:11.   [g]Cf. Hos. 1:10.

[2]Make room [in your hearts] for us. We wronged no one. We corrupted no one. We took advantage of no one. [3]I am not saying this to condemn you. Indeed, I have previously said you are in our hearts so deeply that we would die with you or live with you. [4]I have great confidence in you. I am very proud of you.[a] I am very much encouraged [because of the good reports of your conduct[b]]. Even in the midst of all our hardships, I have abundant joy.

[5]Even after we arrived in Macedonia,[c] our bodies had no rest. Many trials beset us—without were conflicts, within were anxieties [concerning affairs at Corinth]. [6]But God, who comforts the downcast, comforted us by the arrival of Titus. [7]And not only by his arrival but by [his report of] the way he was encouraged on account of you. He told of your eager longing [to see us], of your mourning [at the reprimand I sent you], of your zeal in carrying out the measures I suggested.[d] All this made me rejoice still more.

[8]Even though I caused you grief by my letter,[e] I do not regret having sent it—although for a time I was regretful—for I see that the grief my letter caused was only momentary. [9]Now I am glad, not because you were grieved, but because your grief brought you to repentance. You experienced sorrow according to [the purpose of] God, so that our severity was for your good.[f] [10]For godly sorrow produces repentance which is without regret, because it leads to salvation; whereas worldly sorrow results in death.

[11]Now look at what this God-given grief has produced in you: What enthusiasm [to do your duty]! What eagerness [to clear yourselves from blame]! What indignation [against the offenders]! What fear [of impending judgment]! What ardent longing [for our presence]! What zeal [to set things right]! What determination [to achieve justice]! In all these respects[g] you have absolved yourselves from any guilt concerning the matter in question. [12]So although I wrote to you [as I did], it was not [merely] on account of the one who did the wrong, nor [merely] on account of the one who was wronged, but

---

[a]Or, I boast much about you.
[b]Cf. vv. 6-16.
[c]Cf. 2:12-13.
[d]Literally, *of your zeal on my behalf.*
[e]This may be an allusion to a "severe" letter, now lost to us, or it may refer to our 1 Corinthians. Cf. 2 Cor. 2:1-4.
[f]More literally, *so that you might suffer no loss as a result of what we did.*
[g]Literally, *in everything.*

that your devotion [and obedience] to us[h] might be made plain to you in the sight of God. [13]This—the fact that my letter accomplished its purpose—is what brought us comfort.

Moreover, in addition to our own comfort, we rejoiced further at Titus' joy, because his spirit has been set at rest by your unanimity.[i] [14]I had boasted somewhat to him about [the confidence I felt in] you, [and now that he has brought back such a commendable report] I have no reason to be ashamed [of my complimentary remarks]. Just as on every occasion we have spoken the truth to you, so also the boast we made to Titus has proved true. [15]His affection for you is now greater than ever, as he recalls how willing all of you were to do what he requested, and how you received him with respect and honor. [16]I rejoice that in everything I am of good courage in regard to you.

Chapter 8

Now, brothers, let us tell you what God's grace has accomplished in the churches of Macedonia.[a] [2]Although they were severely tested by adversity their abundant joy, even in extreme poverty, has overflowed in a wealth of liberality. [3]For I can assure you that they have given to the utmost of their ability, and even beyond their ability, and have done so voluntarily. [4]They begged us insistently to give them the privilege of taking part in the contribution for the saints [in Judea]. [5]They did far more than we expected. However, they first gave themselves to the Lord and to us by the will of God.

[6]And so we have urged Titus that, since he was the one who began [the collection among you], he should [return to Corinth and] lead you to the completion of this benevolent project. [7]Just as you abound in everything else—in faith and eloquence and knowledge and ardent enthusiasm and in our common bond of love—see that you abound also in the grace of generosity.

[8]I say this not as a command but to challenge you by mentioning the diligence of others, and to test the genuineness of your love.

[h]Some manuscripts read, our devotion to you.
[i]Literally, by you all.
[a]Cf. Acts 16:12ff; 17:1-4, 10-12.

9For you are aware of the unselfishness[b] shown by our Lord Jesus Christ: Because of you he became poor, while being rich, in order that you, by means of his poverty, might become rich. 10And in this matter [of the relief fund] I offer only a suggestion, which is all expediency requires in your case, inasmuch as you led the way a year ago, not only by contributing as you did but by being the first to propose that such action be taken.

11Now, with the same readiness you had in being willing [to start the project], carry it through to completion—finish it according to your means. 12For where there is willingness, [a gift] is acceptable [to God] in proportion to what [a person] may have and not in proportion to what he does not have. 13This is not to say that relief should be sent to others and distress brought upon you, but that responsibilities should be equalized. 14At the present time your abundance [may supply] what they lack, so that [if the circumstances are reversed] their abundance [may supply] what you lack. In this way reciprocity may be achieved, 15even as it stands written, "He who gathered much did not have too much, and he who gathered little did not have too little."[c]

16Now thanks be to God for instilling in the heart of Titus the same interest [that I feel] in your well-being. 17Not only did he consent to our request but he is so eager to assist that he is returning to you of his own choice. 18With him we are sending the brother whose praise in the [service of the] gospel has spread through all the churches.

19And not only that, but he has been selected by the churches to travel with us in this benevolent work we are promoting for the glory of the Lord himself and [to indicate] our own readiness [to share]. 20We are taking these precautions in the hope that no one will be able to blame us regarding the way we manage the liberal sum entrusted to our care. 21Our intention is to act honorably not only in the sight of God but in the sight of men.

22Also, along with them we are sending a third brother, whose diligence we have often proved in many matters, and who is now more enthusiastic than ever on account of his great confidence in you. 23Regarding Titus, he is my associate and fellow worker among

---

bLiterally, *the grace.*   cCf. Exod. 16:18.

you. As for the [other two] brothers, they are messengers of the [participating] churches, and men who honor Christ. 24So demonstrate your love to them, and let them see that we were right in boasting about you before the churches.

Chapter 9

It is superfluous for me to be writing to you about the collection for the saints. 2I know, of course, of your willingness to help, and I am continually boasting about it to the Macedonians, telling them, "Achaia has been ready to contribute since last year." And your zeal has been a strong incentive to many of them. 3Nevertheless I am sending the brothers[a] [to you] so that our boasting about you may not be in vain on this point, and that you may be as well prepared as I have said you would be.

4Otherwise if some Macedonians come with me and find the collection not completed, it will humiliate us—not to mention you—after having expressed so much confidence. 5So [to preclude any such embarrassment] I thought it necessary to urge the brothers to visit you ahead of me, and make sure in advance that the contribution you promised is completed, so that [when I arrive] it may be ready as a willing gift and not as a reluctant one.

6Remember this principle: He who sows scantily will reap scantily. He who sows generously will reap generously. 7Each person [should give] just as he has planned in his heart, not with regret, not from compulsion. For God loves a joyful giver. 8And God is able to make every gracious benefit abound for you, so that at all times and in all circumstances you may have plenty for your own needs, and be able to contribute to every worthy cause,[b] 9just as it stands written, "He scattered abroad, he gave to the poor. His righteousness continues forever."[c] 10And the One who provides seed for the planter and bread for eating will provide you with adequate resources, and multiply them and increase the harvest of your righteousness.

11Being enriched in everything, you will be able to show unbounded liberality [and, when your gifts are] distributed by us, God

---

aViz., Titus and his two colleagues (cf. 8:18, 22).
bLiterally, *to abound in every good work.*   cCf. Ps. 112:9.

will be praised. [12]The service you are rendering not only supplies the needs of the saints by adding to [the funds contributed by the other congregations[d]], but it overflows in many thanksgivings to God.

[13]The proof of your profession, as demonstrated by this benevolence, will cause [the recipients] to give glory to God for your obedience to the gospel of Christ and for the generosity of your contribution[e] to them and to God's cause in general. [14]They will pray for you and be drawn toward you because of the exceeding grace of God which is upon you. [15]Thanks be to God for his indescribable Gift!

Chapter 10

Now I, Paul, personally appeal to you by the gentleness and mildness exemplified by Christ—I who [so some say] am humble in manner when present with you but bold in language when absent from you—[2]yes I beg you not to force me [when I come] to use the stern measures against any of you I intend to take against certain ones who accuse us of acting from mere human motives. [3]Of course we are subject to the limitations of humanity, but we are not engaged in worldly battles.

[4]For the weapons of our warfare are not ordinary, natural ones, but, made effective with God's help, they have the power to demolish strongholds, to refute arguments, [5]and [to overthrow] every antagonism that lifts itself against the knowledge of God, and to lead captive every plot and make it subservient to Christ. [6]And when your obedience is complete, we are ready to punish any who still refuse to obey.

[7]Look at the facts—at those things which are before your eyes![a] Whoever is convinced that he belongs to Christ should do some careful thinking about himself and understand that we belong to Christ just as much as he does. [8]Even if I were to boast somewhat at length concerning our authority—which the Lord gave us to build you up and not to pull you down—there is adequate ground for my boasting. [9]I do not want you to think that I would intimidate you by means of my letters. [10]"His letters," somebody alleges, "are weighty and

---

[d]Cf. 1 Cor. 16:1; 2 Cor. 8:1ff.; 9:2.   [e]Or, for the sincerity of your fellowship.
[a]Or, Are you influenced only by outward appearances?

bold, but his personal appearance is unimpressive and his speech is contemptible." [11]Let anyone who engages in such talk be assured that whatever we say by our letters when we are absent will be substantiated by our deeds when we are present.

[12]Actually we do not dare[b] to classify or compare ourselves with certain people who speak highly of themselves. They lack good judgment when they measure themselves by one another, and compare themselves with one another. [13]We, however, do not make excessive claims but keep within the limits of the sphere of activity which God assigned to us—and these limits reach far enough to include you.

[14]For we are not overextending ourselves, as though you were not in our area of responsibility. As a matter of fact, we were the first to reach you with the gospel of Christ. [15]We make no fanciful boasts in regard to fields where others have labored. But we hope that, as your faith increases, our range of influence may be greatly enlarged through your aid, [16]so that we shall be able to evangelize the regions west of Achia,[c] without claiming credit for what has already been accomplished in another man's territory. [17]But whoever boasts, let him boast in the Lord.[d] [18]For it is not the man who commends himself who is approved, but the one whom the Lord commends.

Chapter 11

I wish you would bear with a little foolishness on my part. Yes, do be patient with me. [2]For I have a personal interest in you—I am jealous for you with a jealousy that has its source in God. I betrothed you to one husband, to present you as a pure virgin to Christ. [3]But I am afraid that in some way, as the serpent completely deceived Eve by his cunning,[a] your thoughts may be led astray from the pure and wholehearted devotion [which should be maintained] toward Christ.

[4]For when someone comes along and proclaims another Jesus than the one we preached, or you receive a spirit different from the one you have received, or a gospel different from that which you have acknowledged, your toleration is indeed surprising! [5]Actually, I think

---

[b]Paul here speaks ironically as he refers to the pretensions of imposters.
[c]Literally, *the regions beyond you.* Cf. Rom. 15:18-29.
[d]Cf. Jer. 9:23-24.   [a]Cf. Gen. 3:1ff.

that I am in no way inferior to those [who claim to be] "super apostles."[b] [6]If I am not a polished orator, I am not lacking in knowledge, and I have always been able to make my meaning clear to you.

[7]Did I do wrong in humbling myself by working for a living[c] in order that you might be exalted, because I preached the good news of God's gospel to you without pay? [8]I robbed other congregations by accepting support from them so that I might serve you! [9]When I was in your midst, and needed anything, I did not put pressure on any of you. My needs were fully supplied by the brothers who came from Macedonia. So I kept myself from being a burden to you in any way, and this will continue to be my practice. [10]The truth of Christ is in me, consequently this boast [regarding my practice of preaching without charge] shall not be silenced anywhere in Achaia. [11]Why? Because I do not love you? God knows [I do love you].

[12]But I will continue my present policy [of self-support] in order that I may expose the character of those who want an opportunity [to make it appear that they work as unselfishly as we do][d] Let such boasters be judged by the same criteria as we are. [13]Actually, such men are false apostles, deceitful workmen, masquerading as apostles of Christ. [14]And no wonder, for Satan himself masquerades as an angel of light. [15]Hence it is not surprising[e] that his servants also disguise themselves as ministers of righteousness. But their final outcome will be in accordance with their deeds.

[16]Again I say, let no one think that I am really foolish; but if you do think so, at least give me the consideration you would a fool, in order that I may have my turn to boast a little. [17]This sort of talk has no basis in the example of the Lord. I speak as a fool might speak in boasting so confidently. [18]Since many are boasting from the standpoint of natural distinctions, I will do likewise. [19]You have a remarkable tolerance for unwise people, because you are so wise yourselves![f] [20]You even put up with it when someone[g] brings you into bondage, or preys upon you, or defrauds you, or assumes an attitude of superiority, or strikes you in the face! [21]To my shame, I must admit that we were too weak [to abuse you like that]!

---

bA sarcastic reference to the self-sytled "apostles" who were causing trouble in the congregation at Corinth (cf. v. 13). The Twelve are not meant, for Paul held them in high esteem (cf. Gal. 2:9).
cCf. Acts 18:1-4. dLiterally, *in the thing in which they boast.*
eLiterally, *it is no great thing.*
fPaul uses strong irony in this passage. gLiterally, *if anyone.*

But in whatever respect anyone may make strong claims—although it is foolish for me to say this—I can do likewise. 22Hebrews are they? So am I! Israelites are they? So am I! Abraham's descendants are they? So am I! 23Christ's ministers are they? I am speaking as if I were out of my mind, but I am far more [a minister of Christ than they, and my record of service shows it]: with far more extensive labors, far more imprisonments, floggings beyond bounds, nearly losing my life many times. 24Five times at the hands of the Jews I received the maximum of thirty-nine lashes.ʰ 25Three times I was beaten with rods. Once I was stoned. Three times I was shipwrecked. I spent a night and a day adrift in the deep.

26I have made many journeys amid dangers from rivers, dangers from bandits, dangers from my own countrymen, dangers from pagan peoples, dangers in the city, dangers in the wilderness, dangers at sea, dangers among so-called brothers. 27I have experienced toil and hardship, often going without sleep. I have endured famine and thirst, at times almost dying of hunger. I have known cold and what it means to be without adequate clothing. 28And not to mention other things, there is the daily pressure of my concern for all the churches. 29When someone is weak, do I not sympathize with him?ⁱ When someone is enticed [into sin], does not my heart burn [for his restoration]?

30If I am forced to boast, I will boast of the things that show how weak I am! 31The God and Father of the Lord Jesus Christ, he who is blessed forever, knows that I do not lie. 32At Damascus, the Ethnarch under King Aretas kept a close watch throughout the city of the Damascenes in an effort to seize me. 33But through an opening in the wall I was lowered in a rope-basket, and so eluded his hands.ʲ

Chapter 12

There is nothing to be gained by boasting, but since I am forced to it, I will go on to [mention] visions and revelations disclosed by the Lord. 2I know a man in Christ who, fourteen years ago—whether he was in the body or out of the body, I do not know, God knows—

ʰCf. Deut. 25:3.   ⁱLiterally, *Who is weak, and I am not weak?*
ʲCf. Acts 9:23-25.

that man was transported into the third heaven. [3]I know that this man—whether he was in the body or apart from the body, I do not know, God knows—[4]was transported into Paradise and heard things so profound that no human being can relate them. [5]Concerning such an experience I will boast, but on my own behalf I will not boast, except with regard to my weaknesses.

[6]And yet if I do choose to boast, I shall not be foolish, for I shall speak the truth. However, I refrain [from any further recital of my unique experiences] so that no one may think more highly of me than is warranted by what he himself sees me do or hears me say. [7]And to prevent me from being unduly elated because of the extraordinary character of the revelations, I was given a thorn[a] for my flesh, an agent of Satan to harass me, to keep me from being unduly elated. [8]Three times I prayed to the Lord about this, asking that it might depart from me. [9]But he has replied to me, "My grace is sufficient for you. For my power exhibits itself most effectively through people who realize they are weak."

Most gladly, therefore, I will boast all the more in my weaknesses, so that the power of Christ may rest upon me.[b] [10]That is why I rejoice in weaknesses, in insults, in hardships, in persecutions and desperate circumstances on behalf of Christ; for whenever I am weak, then I am strong.

[11]I have become foolish [by the way I have been boasting]. But you have driven me to it. Actually, I ought to have been commended by you. For in no way was I inferior to the "super apostles,"[c] even though I am nothing. [12]The distinguishing marks of a genuine apostle[d] were demonstrated courageously and consistently[e] [during my ministry] among you with signs and wonders and powerful deeds. [13]How, then, were you treated worse than the rest of the churches, except that I myself did not put pressure on you [for my personal upkeep]? Forgive me this wrong![f]

[14]Now this is the third time I am ready to visit you, and I will not put any [financial] pressure on you. I do not want your possessions —I want you. It is not the obligation of children to provide for their parents, but parents for their children. [15]So I will gladly spend [what

---

[a]Cf. Num. 33:55; Ezek. 28:24.
[b]Literally, *may cover me like a tent.* [c]Cf. 11:5.
[d]Literally, *of the apostle.* [e]Literally, in all *perseverance.* [f]Strong irony.

I have], and pour out my very self, in behalf of your souls. Can it be that the more intensely I love you the less I am loved? 16You agree that I was never a burden to you. Nevertheless, [some charge that I am] a cunning person who tricked you [into exploitation by means of others*g*]. 17Have I ever taken advantage of you through any of the representatives I have sent to you? 18I urged Titus [to visit you], and with him I sent the brother.*h* Surely Titus took no advantage of you, did he? Did not he and I show the same attitude?*i* Were we not guided by the same principles?*j*

19I hope you do not imagine that all this time we have been defending ourselves to you. It is in relation to Christ that we are speaking, before God, and everything [we are saying], beloved, is directed toward your spiritual upbuilding. 20For I am afraid that when I come I may find you are not what I want you to be, and you may find I am what you do not want me to be.*k* [I am afraid] that perhaps [there may be among you] contention, suspicion, ill will, self-seeking, slander, gossip, conceit, disorder. 21And when I come again my God may make me feel ashamed on account of your behavior, and I may have cause to mourn over many who have continued in their past sins and have never repented of the impurity and fornication and debauchery which they have practiced.

Chapter 13

This is the third time I am coming to you. [Remember that the Scripture says], "Any charge must be substantiated by the evidence of two or three witnesses."*a* 2I gave warning when I was with you the second time,*b* and I repeat it now in my absence, saying to those who are guilty of previous sins, and to all the rest, that when I come I will show no leniency.*c* 3You are seeking proof that Christ speaks through me—you will have it then! He [who commissioned me] is not weak in his dealings with you but is powerful in your midst.

---

*g*Implied by context. Apparently critics had accused Paul of scheming to get a personal share of the collection being raised for the poor saints of Judea.
*h*Cf. 8:18.   *i*Or, Were we not motivated by the same Spirit?
*j*Literally, *Did we not walk in the same steps?*
*k*By the latter clause Paul seems to mean, You will not like the corrective action I may have to take. Cf. 10:2-6.
*a*Cf. Deut. 19:15.   *b*Cf. 2:1.   *c*Cf. 1:23.

⁴It is true that he was crucified due to [his assumption of our] weakness,*d* yet he lives by the power of God. So it is with us: We are weak in relation to him, but we shall share in his life, through [the expression of] God's power, in dealing with you.

⁵You should be examining your own selves to see if you are in the faith! Keep putting yourselves to the test! Surely you know yourselves well enough to recognize that Jesus Christ dwells in you, unless—which I am certain is not the case*e*—you cannot pass the test. ⁶I hope you will recognize that we are not counterfeits. ⁷Now we pray to God that you may do nothing wrong—not in order that we may appear approved, but that you may do what is excellent even if we seem to be disapproved. ⁸[You have nothing to fear if you abide in the truth], for we cannot do anything against the truth—we can only promote it. ⁹Actually, we rejoice at the loss of an occasion for using our apostolic authority when you require no exercise of it.*f* And this is our prayer, that you may be made complete.*g*

¹⁰I am writing these things while I am away from you, so that when I arrive I may not have to deal sharply with you in accordance with the authority which the Lord gave me for the purpose of building you up and not for the purpose of tearing you down.

¹¹Finally, brothers, farewell.*h* Keep striving for what you ought to be.*i* Follow my admonitions. Cultivate unanimity of thought. Live in peace, and the God of love and peace will be with you. ¹²Greet one another with a holy kiss. All the saints send you their greetings.

¹³The grace of the Lord Jesus Christ and the love of God and the fellowship of the Holy Spirit be with you all!

---

*d*Cf. 8:9.
*e*Indicated by *mēti,* interrogative particle which implies a negative answer. Cf. 12:18.
*f*Literally, *we rejoice when we ourselves are weak if only you yourselves are strong.*
*g*Or, made strong; or, spiritually equipped.   *h*Or, rejoice.
*i*Or, for completion; or, to be fully equipped.

GALATIANS

Chapter 1

Paul, an apostle—not from men nor by human agency, but through Jesus Christ and God the Father who raised him from the dead—²and all the brothers who are with me, to the churches in Galatia: ³Grace to you, and peace, from God your Father and [from] the Lord Jesus Christ, ⁴who gave himself for our sins in order to deliver us from the present wicked world according to the plan of our God and Father. ⁵To him be the glory for ever and ever! Amen.

⁶I am certainly amazed that you are so quickly in the process of moving away from him who called you by the gracious favor of Christ, [and turning] to another gospel. ⁷Actually, there is no other gospel. But there are certain people who are troubling you and trying to pervert the gospel of the Christ. ⁸Now even if we, or an angel from heaven, preach to you as gospel a message not in accord with that which we preached to you, let him be accursed! ⁹As we said before, so now I say again: If anyone is preaching to you as gospel a message not in accord with that which you have received, let him be accursed!

¹⁰Am I now trying to gain the approval of men or of God? Do I seek to please men? If I were still trying to please men, I would not be a servant of Christ. ¹¹I want you to know, brothers, that the gospel which was preached by me is no human message. ¹²Indeed, I did not receive it from man, nor was I taught it by anyone, but I received it through revelation from Jesus Christ. ¹³You have heard of my manner of life when I was in Judaism, how violently I used to persecute the church of God and kept trying to destroy it.

¹⁴I was advancing in the Jewish religion beyond many of my contemporaries, because of my extreme zeal for the traditions of my forefathers. ¹⁵But when it pleased him, who from my birth had set me apart and called me by his grace, ¹⁶to reveal his Son in me that

I might preach the good news about him among the Gentiles, immediately, instead of deliberating with any human being [17]or going
up to Jerusalem to confer with those who were apostles before me,
I went away into Arabia, and on my return came back to Damascus.

[18]Three years later I went up to Jerusalem to get acquainted with
Cephas, and I remained with him fifteen days. [19]But I did not see
any of the other apostles except James, the Lord's brother. [20](In
writing these things to you, behold, before God, I am giving an
exact account of what happened.) [21]After that, I went into the regions
of Syria and Cilicia.[a] [22]I was still not known personally by Christ's
congregations in Judea.[b] [23]But they kept hearing, "He who used to
persecute us is now preaching the faith which he formerly attempted
to destroy." [24]And they gave praise to God because of the change
in me.

Chapter 2

After an interval of fourteen years I again went up to Jerusalem,
accompanied by Barnabas, and I also took Titus with me. [2]I went up
by divine direction, and I put before them the gospel as I preach it
among the Gentiles. I had discussions privately with the leaders,
[for I wanted to make sure] that my ministry would not be hindered
by anyone.

[3]Although Titus who was with me was a Greek, he was not com-
pelled to be circumcised. [4][His circumcision was demanded by] the
false brothers who entered secretly—men of such character that they
sneaked in to spy on the freedom we enjoy in Christ Jesus. Their
objective was to bring us into bondage. [5]But not for a moment did
we yield to their demand. [We remained steadfast] in order that the
truth of the gospel might prevail for your benefit.

[6]The men who were considered to be leaders—what sort of persons they were makes no difference to me: God regards no man's
outward appearance—indeed the men of repute added nothing to my
message. [7]On the contrary, when they saw that I had been entrusted
with the gospel for the uncircumcised, just as Peter [had been en-

---

[a]Cf. Acts 9:30; 15:23, 41.
[b]Excluding Jerusalem, where Paul was known personally. Cf. Acts 9:26-29.

trusted with it] for the circumcised [8](for he who made Peter's apostle-ship effective among the Jews also made mine effective among the Gentiles)—[9]when they became aware of the favor granted to me, James and Cephas and John, who were considered to be pillars, gave to Barnabas and me the right hand of fellowship, agreeing that we should go to the Gentiles, and they to the Jews. [10]They suggested only that we keep remembering the poor, the very thing I was eager to do.

[11]Now when Cephas came to Antioch I opposed him to his face, pointing out that he stood condemned by his inconsistent conduct.[a] [12]For before certain men came from James, he used to eat with the Gentiles. But when they arrived, he began to draw back and to separate himself [from the Gentiles] because he was afraid of offending those who advocated circumcision.[b] [13]And the rest of the Jewish believers joined him in the pretense[c] [that it was not right to eat with Gentiles]. Even Barnabas was carried away by their pretension.

[14]As soon as I saw that they were not acting according to the truth of the gospel, I said to Cephas in the presence of them all: "If you, being a Jew, live like a Gentile and not like a Jew, how can you try to compel the Gentiles to act like Jews?" [15]We are Jews by nature and not Gentile sinners. [16]But we know that a person is not declared righteous on the basis of any works of law, but only through faith in Christ Jesus. And we ourselves placed trust in Christ Jesus in order that we might be declared righteous on the basis of faith in Christ, and not on the basis of obedience to law. For on the basis of works of law no human being shall be declared righteous.[d]

[17]But if, while we are seeking to be declared righteous in Christ, we ourselves also are found to be sinners, does this make Christ an agent of sin? Absolutely not! [18]But if I build up again the very things which I have torn down, I prove myself a transgressor. [19]Actually, through the operation of the Law, I myself died to the Law in order that I might become alive to God.[e] I have been crucified with Christ.

[20]My former self is no longer in control, but Christ lives in me. The life I now live in the body I am living by faith in the Son of

---

aCf. Acts 15:6-11.   bCf. Acts 11:2ff.   cLiterally, *played the hypocrite with him.*
dCf. Ps. 142.2 (Septuagint).
eThe Law made impossible demands which provoked those under it to sin. Christ alone satisfies the requirements of the Law and by grace saves the sinner who places trust in him. Cf. Rom. 7:4ff., 8:1-4.

God, who loved me and gave himself in my behalf. [21]I do not make ineffective the grace of God. For if righteousness could be achieved by means of any legal system at all,[f] then Christ died unnecessarily.

Chapter 3

O foolish Galatians, who has tricked you—you before whose very eyes Jesus Christ was so vividly pictured as crucified?[a] [2]Let me ask you just one question: Did you receive the Spirit as a result of works of law, or as a result of believing the message you heard? [3]How can you be so foolish? You began [your new life] by the Spirit. Are you now trying to complete it by ceremonial observances? [4]Have you suffered so many things in vain—if they have really been in vain?

[5]When God provides you with the Spirit and performs mighty deeds among you, is it because of works of law,[b] or because you believed the message you heard? [6]Just as [it is written], "Abraham believed God, and his faith was counted to him for righteousness."[c]

[7]Hence you should realize that the real sons of Abraham are the people of faith. [8]Now the Scripture, having anticipated that God would declare the Gentiles righteous on the condition of faith, announced in advance the good news to Abraham in the words, "Through you shall all the nations be blessed."[d] [9]Consequently those who have faith are blessed in association with Abraham the believer.

[10]Actually, all who depend on works prescribed by law are under a curse. For it stands written, "Cursed is everyone who does not continue in all the precepts that are written in the book of the Law, to perform them."[e] [11]On the other hand, it is clear that no man is declared righteous before God on any legal grounds, because [the Scripture says] "The righteous shall live by faith."[f]

[12]But the Law is not based on faith. It declares, "The man who does these things will live by doing them."[g] [13]Christ delivered us from the curse of the Law, by taking the curse upon himself in our behalf—for it stands written, "Cursed is everyone who is hanged on a tree"[h]—[14]in order that the blessing promised to Abraham might

---

[f]Anarthrous *nomos* includes the entire scope of law, Mosaic and otherwise.
[a]The perfect passive participle, *estaurōmenos, having been crucified,* emphasizes the fact of Jesus' crucifixion and its permanent results.   [b]Cf. Gal. 2:16; 3:2.
[c]Cf. Gen. 15:6; Rom. 4:3.   [d]Gen. 12:3.   [e]Deut. 27:26.   [f]Hab. 2:4.
[g]Lev. 18:5.   [h]Deut. 21:23.

come to the Gentiles through Jesus Christ, so that through faith we might receive the promise of the Spirit.

[15]Brothers, let me use an illustration from ordinary procedure: Even when a human agreement has been ratified, no one can set it aside or change it. [16]Now the promises were spoken to Abraham and to his descendant. It does not say, "And to the descendants," as if referring to many. It says, "And to your descendant," referring to one, who is Christ.[i] [17]What I mean is this: The agreement previously ratified by God [to Abraham] cannot be annulled and its promise invalidated by the Law, which came into being four hundred and thirty years later. [18]For if the inheritance is conditioned on law, it cannot be based on promise. But by means of promise God granted it to Abraham as a free gift.

[19]Then why was the Law given? It was added to make men aware of their transgressions, [and it was to function] until the coming of the Descendant concerning whom the promise had been made. It was enacted through the agency of angels by the hand of an intermediary.[j] [20]An intermediary acts for other persons [as did Moses in receiving the Law for Israel], but God acted directly [in making the promise to Abraham].

[21]Does it follow that the Law was contrary to God's promises? Not at all! Certainly if there had been given any kind of law that was capable of imparting life, then truly righteousness would have been realized by means of law. [22]But the Scripture has locked up together the whole world[k] under the condemnation of sin, so that the promise conditioned on faith in Jesus Christ might be given to those who believe.

[23]But before this faith came, we were kept under the custody of law in anticipation of the faith that was to be revealed. [24]Thus the Law served as a pedagogue[l] to bring us to Christ, in order that we might be declared righteous on the basis of faith.

---

[i]According to Paul, the Hebrew collective singular substantive, *zerà, seed,* of Genesis 13:15; 17:8, involves the Messiah (cf. 22:18). The promises made to Abraham apply to Christ in a special way, for as Abraham's Descendant Christ is the Representative and Head of the new Israel. Cf. Gal. 6:16.

[j]The reference is to Moses. Cf. Exod. 31:18; 32:19. [k]Cf. Rom. 3:9; 11:32.

[l]The Greek noun *paidagōgos, a child-leader,* designates a person of responsibility, usually a slave, appointed by Greek and Roman families of means to have general charge of a boy during the years from about six to sixteen. One duty of the pedagogue was to lead the child to his teacher. This illustrates the purpose of the Mosaic Law which, like an attendant, was meant to point the Jewish people to the Christ.

25But now that the faith has come, we are no longer under [the custody of a pedagogue. 26For all of you are God's sons through your[m] faith in Christ Jesus. 27Indeed, as many of you as were baptized in relation to[n] Christ have clothed yourselves with Christ. 28[From a spiritual standpoint], there is neither Jew nor Greek, there is neither slave nor freeman, there is neither male nor female. As believers, you are all one in Christ Jesus. 29And since you belong to Christ, you are Abraham's true descendants[o]—you are heirs of everything included in the promise.

Chapter 4

What I mean is this: So long as the heir is a child, he is no different from a slave, although he is owner of the entire estate. 2But he is under tutors and property-managers until the time previously set by his father. 3So it was with us: when we were in spiritual childhood, we were held in bondage to the elementary ideas of the world. 4But when the proper time came, God sent forth his Son who was born of a woman, and who became subject to law, 5to redeem those under law, so that we might receive our sonship.

6And because you are sons, God has sent forth the Spirit of his Son into our hearts, motivating us to exclaim,[a] "O God, our Father." 7So you[b] are no longer a slave but a son. And because you are a son, [you are] also an heir through [the act of] God.

8In your earlier experience, when you had no knowledge of God, you were enslaved to deities which have no real existence.[c] 9But now that you have come to know God, or rather are known by God, how can you turn back to those weak and worthless elementary notions, and choose to be in bondage to them all over again? 10You are meticulously observing days and months and certain seasons and years! 11I am very much concerned about you—I am afraid that I may have labored among you in vain.

---

[m]Or, through this faith.   [n]Or, because of trust in Christ. Cf. Rom. 6:3.
[o]Or, offspring, a collective singular noun, applied in this context to all persons who place trust in Jesus Christ.
[a]Literally, exclaiming. Cf. Rom. 8:15.
[b]The change to the singular emphasizes the fact that each believer is a son and an heir.   [c]Literally, those which by nature are not gods.

[12]Brothers, I beg of you, become as I am, for I became like you.[d] You have not done me any wrong. [13]You remember it was a physical affliction of mine that gave rise to the circumstances under which I first preached the gospel to you.[e] [14]Even though my physical appearance was repulsive, you did not scorn or despise me, but received me as an angel of God, as if I were Christ Jesus.

[15]What has become of your original enthusiasm?[f] Indeed, I can bear witness that, had it been possible, you would have torn out your eyes and given them to me! [16]Have I become your enemy by telling you the truth? [17]The Judaizers[g] are giving you a lot of attention, but their motive is dishonorable. They want to shut you out [from the liberty of the gospel] so that you will defect to their point of view. [18]Of course it is honorable to be sought after in a good cause, always, and not only when I am with you. [19]My dear children—you for whom I travail again in birth pangs until Christ's likeness is completely formed in you!—[20]I wish I were there with you right now, and could reason with you in the proper tone of voice,[h] for I am perplexed about you.

[21]Tell me, you who want to be under law, do you not understand [the significance of] the Law? [22]For it stands written that Abraham had two sons, one by a slave girl and the other by a free woman. [23]The son of the slave girl was born according to the ordinary course of nature,[i] but the son of the free woman was born in fulfillment of God's promise.[j]

[24]Now, speaking allegorically,[k] these women are two covenants. The one, proceeding from Mount Sinai, brings forth children for slavery. This is Hagar. [25]Now Hagar represents Mount Sinai in Arabia [where the Law was given], and corresponds to the present Jerusalem which along with her children continues in bondage [to the Law]. [26]But the heavenly Jerusalem is free, and she[l] is our mother.

---

[d]The Apostle is making a strong plea to his readers—Gentiles who were originally without the Judaistic system—not to regress to the bondage of legalism. He bases his appeal on the ground that he, who was formerly under that legalism, had forsaken it and put himself, in relation to it, on the same level with them.   [e]Cf. Acts 13:13ff.

[f]Or, your self-congratulation.

[g]Literally, they.

[h]Literally, and could change my tone.   [i]Cf. Gen. 16:1ff.

[j]Literally, through the promise. Cf. Gen. 15:4; 17:19.

[k]Literally, which things are allegorized.

[l]The indefinite relative pronoun, hētis, emphasizes the qualitative aspect of the new Jerusalem.

[27]Indeed it stands written, "Rejoice, O childless woman that bearest not! Break forth and cry aloud, thou that hast no birthpangs! For the desolate woman has more children than she who has a husband![m]

[28]Now you, [n]brothers, like Isaac, are children born in fulfillment of a divine promise. [29]In those days the son[o] born according to the ordinary course of nature used to persecute the one born by the power of the Spirit, and the situation is the same now. [30]But what does the Scripture say? "Cast out the slave girl and her son. For the son of the slave girl shall in no way whatsoever share the inheritance with the son of the free woman."[p] [31]So, brothers, we are not children of a slave girl, but of the free woman.

Chapter 5

Christ has liberated us that we might enjoy freedom. Therefore keep standing fast, and be not again entangled in any kind of a yoke of bondage. [2]Listen carefully: I, Paul, say to you that if you permit yourselves to be circumcised [with the idea that it is necessary for righteousness], Christ will be of no benefit to you.

[3]I want to make it perfectly plain:[a] Every man who submits to circumcision is obligated to obey the whole Law. [4]If you try to achieve righteousness by means of law, you sever your relationship to Christ—you have abandoned his grace. [5]But we, in the Spirit, on the basis of faith, are eagerly awaiting [the consummation of] the hope which is the fruit of righteousness. [6]Indeed, in Christ Jesus neither circumcision nor uncircumcision has any merit. What matters is faith that expresses itself through love.

[7]You were making excellent progress! Who has interfered to keep you from obeying the truth? [8]The influence [to which you are conceding] is not from him who calls you. [9]A little yeast ferments all the dough.[b] [10]For my part, I am persuaded in the Lord with regard to you, that you will not allow erroneous views to circulate any further.[c] The one who is troubling you, whoever he may be, will have to bear the penalty.

---

[m]Isa. 54:1.   [n]Some manuscripts read, *hēmeis, we.*
[o]Literally, *the one.*   [p]Gen. 21:10.   [a]Literally, *And I again declare.*
[b]Perhaps a proverbial saying. Cf. 1 Cor. 5:6.
[c]Literally, *that you will think nothing other.*

[11]Brothers, if I still preach circumcision [as some claim I do when it suits my purpose[d]], why am I still being persecuted? If I were preaching circumcision,[e] then [the message about] the cross would cease to arouse opposition. [12]Those who are trying to unsettle you might as well [carry out the full implications of their dogma and] emasculate themselves![f]

[13]Indeed, brothers, you were called to freedom. Only do not use this freedom as an opportunity for selfish expression, but through love[g] serve one another. [14]For the whole Law is summarized in this one statement: "You must love your neighbor as yourself."[h] [15]But if you prey upon one another like wild animals, be careful or you will be destroyed by one another.

[16]Now I say, Walk by the [guidance of the] Spirit, and you will not carry out the cravings of the old nature. [17]For the desire of the old nature is contrary to that of the Spirit, and the [desire] of the Spirit is contrary to that of the old nature. These are opposed to each other, and this conflict tends to prevent you from doing what you want to do. [18]But if you are led by the Spirit, you are not under any legal system.

[19]Now the works of the old nature are well known and include, for example, sexual vice, impurity, indecency, [20]idolatry, sorcery, enmity, strife, jealousy, uncontrolled temper, selfish ambition, dissension, faction-making, [21]ill will, drunkenness, carousing, and the like. I warn you plainly, as I have done previously, that people who do such things shall not inherit the kingdom of God.

[22]But the fruit produced by the Spirit is love,[i] joy, peace, long-suffering, kindness, generosity, faith,[j] [23]gentleness, self-control. Against such things there is no law. [24]And those who belong to Christ Jesus have crucified the old nature with its dispositions and cravings. [25]If we are living in the sphere of the Spirit [our conduct should verify that fact]. Let us continue walking [in an orderly manner with our lives regulated] by the Spirit. [26]Let us stop striving after empty honor, and not provoke one another to strife, or regard one another with envy.

---

[d]Cf. Acts 16:3.
[e]Literally, consequently.
[f]This ironical statement reflects Paul's disgust with the legalists.
[g]Greek, agapē.   [h]Lev. 19:18.
[i]Greek, agapē.   [j]Or, faithfulness.

Chapter 6

Brothers, if a man is actually overtaken in some misdeed, you who are spiritual restore him in an attitude of meekness, keeping a close watch on yourself. For you also may fall into temptation, 2Bear one another's burdens, and thus you will fulfill the law of Christ. 3Indeed, if anyone thinks he is something when he is nothing, he deludes himself. 4But let each one keep testing his own work, and then he can rejoice about his own accomplishments instead of claiming credit for what someone else has done. 5For every man must shoulder his own responsibility.

6Let the person who is being instructed in the Word share with his instructor in all good things. 7Cease being led astray. No one sneers at God [and gets by with it], for whatever a man sows, that very thing he will also reap. 8The man who sows in the realm of his old nature will from the old nature reap ruin. But he who sows in the realm of the Spirit will from the Spirit reap life eternal. 9And let us not lose heart in doing what is good, for at the proper season we shall reap if we do not relax our efforts. 10So then, as we have opportunity, let us do good to all men, especially to those who are devoted to the faith.

11Notice the large letters with which I write to you in my own handwriting. 12Those who are trying to compel you to receive circumcision want to make an impressive showing before men, only to avoid suffering persecution for the cross of Christ. 13Actually, those who are circumcised fail to observe the Law themselves. They want you to receive circumcision in order that they may boast over your subjection to outward rites.

14But as for me, may I never boast except in the cross of our Lord Jesus Christ, by which the world has been crucified to me, and I to the world. 15For neither circumcision nor uncircumcision is anything of importance. The only thing that counts is a transformation of character. 16And as many as live by this principle, peace and mercy be upon them—even upon the Israel of God.

17From now on, let no one make trouble for me. For I bear in my body the scars[a] [that mark me as a servant] of Jesus.

18May the gracious favor of our Lord Jesus Christ be with your spirit, brothers. Amen.

---

aCf. 2 Cor. 11:24-25.

EPHESIANS

Chapter 1

Paul, an apostle of Christ Jesus by the will of God, to the saints who are at Ephesus, the faithful in Christ Jesus: ²Grace to you and peace from God our Father and the Lord Jesus Christ.

³Blessed be the God and Father of our Lord Jesus Christ, who has blessed us with every spiritual blessing in the heavenly realms in Christ, ⁴even as he chose us for himself before the world's creation, that we should be holy and blameless in his sight. ⁵In love*a* he planned in advance through Jesus Christ for us to become his sons by adoption, according to the good purpose of his will, ⁶that we might praise him for the gracious favor which he has freely bestowed upon us in the Beloved One, ⁷in whom we have redemption through his blood, the forgiveness of our misdeeds, according to the wealth of his grace ⁸which he made abound toward us in complete wisdom and insight, ⁹having made known to us the secret of his intention according to the good pleasure which he purposed in himself,*b* ¹⁰to become effective at the proper time, that all things might be summed up in Christ—the things in heaven and the things on earth—¹¹in him in whom also we were made a heritage.

[This was] planned in advance according to the purpose of him who is working everything in accord with the design of his will, ¹²so that we who were the first to place our hope in Christ might express praise to his glory. ¹³You also, after hearing the word of truth, the gospel of your salvation, and having believed in him, were sealed*c* by the promised Holy Spirit ¹⁴who is the initial installment of our inheritance—the pledge that we shall receive the full possession of what has been purchased for us,*d* that his glory may be praised.

*a*Or, blameless before him in love.
*b*Or, which he planned in him (that is, in Christ).
*c*Or, stamped, marked, or authenticated.
*d*Or, that the redemption [begun in us] will be brought to full and final completion. Cf. 1:7.

[15]That is why, since I heard of the faith[e] in the Lord Jesus which exists among you, and of your love for all the saints, [16]I do not cease to give thanks for you, making mention of you in my prayers, [17]requesting that the God of our Lord Jesus Christ, the Father of glory, may give you the Spirit of wisdom and revelation in the deeper knowledge of himself, [18]that the perception of your heart may be illumined, so that you may know what is the hope to which he has called you, how gloriously rich is the inheritance he has provided for us among the saints, [19]and how exceedingly great is his power for us who believe, in accord with the working of the strength of his might [20]which he demonstrated in Christ when he raised him from the dead and seated him at his right hand in the heavenly realms, [21]far above all rule and authority and power and dominion, and [far above] every name that can be named, not only in the present age but also in that which is to come. [22]And he put everything under his feet,[f] and made him the Head over all things with regard to the church—for the church is his special concern—[23]since by its very nature it is his body, the means of expression for him whose plenitude pervades all creation.

Chapter 2

There was a time when you [Gentiles] were [spiritually] dead due to your misdeeds and sins, [2]in which you indulged in conformity to the ways of this present world order, under the influence of the prince whose domain is spiritual, not material[a]—of the spirit which is still at work in the sons of disobedience. [3]We [Jews] also once lived like that when we were motivated by the cravings of our unregenerate nature, obeying its inclinations and whims, and we were by nature children subject to [divine] wrath like the rest [of mankind].

[4]But God, who is rich in mercy, on account of the great love with which he loved us, [5]even though we were dead due to our misdeeds, made us alive together with Christ—by means of grace you have been saved—[6]and raised us with him and seated us with him in the heavenly realms in Christ Jesus, [7]that in the coming ages he might show

eOr, faithfulness.   /Cf. Ps. 8:6.
aLiterally, *the prince of the power of the lower atmosphere.*

forth the exceeding wealth of his favor in gracious kindness toward us in Christ Jesus. [8]Thus by grace you have been saved through faith. And this [divine act[b] which saves you is] not of yourselves, it is God's free gift. [9]It is not [the result] of any human effort, so no one can ever boast. [10]Actually, we are his workmanship, created in Christ Jesus for [the expression of] good deeds which God previously planned for us to do.[c]

[11]So remember that at one time you who are Gentiles by natural lineage were regarded as the uncircumcised by those who claim the circumcision which is a mere physical act performed by human hands. [12]Do not forget that in those days you were without Christ. You were in a condition of alienation from the special privileges of Israel, and were strangers to the covenants based on the promise. You were without God and without any hope in the world.

[13]But now in Christ Jesus, you who were once far away have been brought near by the blood of Christ. [14]He himself is our Peace. He made the two elements one. By means of his [crucified] body, he broke down the dividing wall, the enmity that separated us, [15]and put an end to the Law with its commandments expressed in decrees, so that in himself he might create out of the two [divisions of humanity] one new people, [thus] making peace; [16]and might reconcile to God both [Jews and Gentiles] in one body through his cross, having slain [their mutual] enmity by means of it.

[17]And he came and proclaimed the good news of peace for you who were far away, and peace for those who were near.[d] [18]Through him we both have access by one Spirit to the Father. [19]Therefore you are no longer strangers and foreigners. You are fellow-citizens with the saints and members of God's household.

[20]You are built upon the foundation laid by the apostles and prophets, Christ Jesus himself being the Cornerstone.[e] [21]In relation to him the entire structure, properly fitted together, rises into a holy temple in the Lord, [22]in whom you yourselves are being built together into a dwelling for God through the Spirit.

---

[b]The Greek demonstrative pronoun, *touto*, is neuter, hence refers to the act of being saved by *grace* (*charis*, feminine) through *faith* (*pistis*, feminine).

[c]It is to be noted that good works do not produce salvation, but that they are the result of it.

[d]Isa. 57:19.

[e]*Akrogōniaios*, literally the stone *at the tip of the angle*. Such a stone, placed at the extreme angle of a building, determines the lines of the entire structure.

Chapter 3

In view of God's unfolding purpose I, Paul, am Jesus Christ's prisoner in behalf of you Gentiles. [2]Surely you have heard of my commission to declare God's grace to you, [3]how by revelation the secret purpose was made known to me, as I have already written briefly.[a] [4]As you read it, you can perceive my insight into the mystery of Christ. [5]In former generations it was not made known to the sons of men as it has now been revealed to his holy apostles and prophets[b] by the Spirit, [6][namely,] that the Gentiles are fellow heirs [with the Jews] and fellow members of the same body, and fellow sharers of the promise realized in Christ Jesus through the gospel, [7]of which I was made a minister by the gift of God's grace bestowed on me by the exercise of his power.

[8]To me, the very least of all saints, was given the privilege of proclaiming to the Gentiles the good news of the unfathomable wealth of Christ, [9]and of showing how the secret purpose, which during the past ages was hidden in God who created all things, is being worked out. [10]It was hidden in order that God's diversified wisdom might now be made known through the church to the rulers and authorities in the heavenly realms [11]in accord with his agelong purpose which he accomplished in Christ Jesus our Lord, [12]in whom we have our boldness and access [to God] with confidence through our faith in him. [13]So I ask you not to lose heart over the hardships [which I am enduring] in your behalf, for [such endurance] results in your benefit.

[14]Because the Gentiles have been brought into God's plan I bend my knees before the Father, [15]from whom the entire family in heaven and on earth is named, [16]that he may grant you, according to the wealth of his glory, to be strengthened with power by his Spirit in the inner man, [17]so that Christ may dwell in your hearts through faith, that being deeply rooted and firmly grounded in [his] love, [18]you—with all the saints—may be fully able to grasp what is the breadth and length and height and depth, [19]and to experience the love of Christ which cannot be fully known, so that you may be filled with all the fullness which God imparts.

---

aCf. 1:9ff.; 2:19ff.   bCf. Acts 15:22ff.

20Now to him who, according to the power at work in us, is able to do far more than anything we can ever ask or imagine—21to him be the glory in the church and in Christ Jesus through all generations, unto endless ages.

Chapter 4

So I, a prisoner for the Lord's sake, urge you to walk in a manner that corresponds with the call which you have received, 2with deep humility and meekness, with longsuffering, bearing with each other in love. 3Be eager to maintain, in the bond of peace, the unity effected by the Spirit. 4There is one body and one Spirit, just as there is one hope based upon your calling. 5There is one Lord, one faith, one baptism. 6There is one God and Father of all, who is above all and through all and in all. 7But to each one of us has been given the favor [of a task to perform[a]], according to the generous measure apportioned by Christ.

8Therefore [the Scripture] says, "When he ascended on high, he led captivity captive, and he gave gifts to men."[b] 9Now the expression, "he ascended," implies that he first descended into the lower regions of the earth.[c] 10The One who descended is the same One who also ascended far above all the heavens, in order that he might complete all things.

11And he commissioned some men apostles, some prophets, some evangelists, some pastors and teachers, 12to equip the saints for the work of service to build up the body of Christ, 13until we all arrive at the unity of the faith and of the clear knowledge of God's Son—to mature manhood, measured by the perfection exemplified in Christ. 14[This is] so that we may be no longer children, tossed like waves and blown about by every wind of doctrine through the trickery of men who are crafty in their methods of deception.

15But let us consistently speak the truth in love, and in every respect grow up in relation to him who is the Head—Christ himself—16from whom the entire body is fitted together and united by means

---

aFor *charis, grace,* in this sense, cf. 3:8; Phil. 1:7.　　bCf. Ps. 68:18.
cOr, into the lower realm which is the earth.

of the various contacts through which it receives sustenance. As each individual part functions properly, the body grows and builds itself up through love.

[17]This I say, therefore, and emphasize with the Lord's authority, that you must no longer live as do the pagans, for their thoughts are futile. [18]Their minds are darkened, and they are in a state of alienation from the life of God, due to the ignorance that is in them because of the hardness of their hearts. [19]They have reached a degraded moral condition in which they have no more awareness of sin, hence have given themselves over to licentiousness, greedily practicing every kind of impurity.

[20]But that is not the way you learned to know Christ—[21]if you really listened to him, as I assume that you did, and in him were taught the truth as it is in Jesus—[22]that you must put off, with your former conduct, the old nature which becomes more and more corrupt as a result of deceptive desires; [23]that your thinking powers must be continually renewed; [24]and that you must put on the new nature which, in accord with [the character of] God, is created in the righteousness and holiness expressive of the truth.

[25]Therefore, having laid aside falsehood, let every man speak the truth to his neighbor, for we are members one of another. [26]Do not allow anger to cause you to commit sin.[d] Make sure the setting sun does not find you resentful. [27]And do not give any opportunity to the devil. [28]Let the person who has been a thief steal no more, but rather let him labor, toiling with his own hands at honorable work, so he may have something to share with those in need.

[29]Let no unwholesome word proceed from your lips, but only whatever conversation is good for edifying, as the occasion requires, that what you say may impart spiritual benefit to the hearers. [30]And do not grieve the Holy Spirit of God, by whom you have been marked[e] with the stamp of divine ownership for the day of [final] redemption. [31]Let all bitterness and hot anger and wrath and violent outbursts and slander, together with every kind of evil, be put away from you completely. [32]Always be kind to one another, deeply compassionate, freely forgiving each other, even as God through Christ graciously forgave you.

[d]Cf. Ps. 4:4.   [e]Cf. 1:13.

Chapter 5

Therefore, follow God's example, as his beloved children, [2]and walk in love, just as Christ loved you and gave himself up for us as a fragrant[a] offering and sacrifice to God.

[3]But sexual vice and every kind of impurity or covetousness should not even be mentioned among you, for such things are out of the question for saints. [4]Obscenity and foolish talk and vulgar jesting are improper. Instead, [let there be] giving of thanks.

[5]Be certain about this: No fornicator, or impure man, or covetous individual—for a covetous person is an idolator—has any inheritance in the kingdom of Christ and of God. [6]Let no one deceive you with empty arguments. It is on account of the vices I have mentioned that God's wrath comes upon the sons of disobedience. [7]So do not be partakers with such people.

[8]Indeed, you were formerly darkness, but now in the Lord you are light. Walk as children of light. [9]For the effects of the light [appear] in everything good and right and true. [10]Continually put things to the test to verify what is well-pleasing to the Lord. [11]Have no fellowship with the unprofitable works of the darkness, but by contrast [let your behavior] expose them.

[12]Actually it is a shame even to speak about the things which are practiced secretly by people who are in darkness. [13]Yet whatever is exposed by the light is made plain, and everything made plain is seen as it really is. [14]Thus we have the statement, "Awake, O thou that sleepest! Stand up from among the dead, and Christ will enlighten you!"[b]

[15]Therefore, see to it that you live carefully—not unwisely, but wisely—[16]making the most of your opportunities, for these are difficult days. [17]So do not be thoughtless, but try to perceive clearly what is the Lord's will. [18]Do not get drunk on wine,[c] a practice which leads to moral ruin. But keep filled with the Spirit. [19]Speak to one another in psalms and hymns and spiritual songs. Sing and make melody from your hearts to the Lord. [20]Always give thanks to God the Father for everything, in the name of our Lord Jesus Christ. [21]Be submissive to one another because of your reverence for Christ.

---

[a]An expression indicating God's acceptance of a sacrifice or presentation. Cf. **Gen.** 8:21; Exod. 29:18; Lev. 1:9; Phil. 4:18.
[b]Cf. Isa. 26:19; 51:17; 52:1; 60:1ff.   [c]Cf. Prov. 23:30.

22Wives, [be submissive] to your own husbands as to the Lord. 23For a husband is the head of his wife, just as Christ is the Head of the church and is himself the Savior of the body. 24As the church is subject to Christ, thus also wives [should be submissive] to their husbands in everything.

25Husbands, cherish your wives with self-sacrificing love, even as Christ loved the church to the extent that he gave himself for her, 26in order that he might sanctify her, having cleansed her by the washing of water in connection with the word,*d* 27that he might present to himself the church in all her beauty, having no moral or spiritual defect of any kind, but that she might be holy and without blemish.

28This is the way husbands ought to love their own wives—with the same concern they have for their own bodies. He who loves his wife loves himself. 29No man ever hated his own body, but he tenderly nourishes and cares for it just as Christ does the church, 30because we are members of his body. 31"Therefore a man is to leave his father and mother, and be united to his wife. And the man and his wife shall be one flesh."*e* 32This is a truth with profound meanings, but I am speaking with reference to [the relationship between] Christ and the church. 33Nevertheless, this also applies to you individually: Let each of you married men love his own wife as [he loves] himself. And let each wife maintain respect for her husband.

Chapter 6

Children, obey your parents in the Lord, for this is right. 2"Honor your father and your mother"—this is a significant commandment accompanied by a promise—3"that it may be well with you and that you may live a long time on the earth."*a* 4Fathers, do not irritate your children, but bring them up tenderly in the discipline and instruction given by the Lord.*b*

5Slaves, obey your earthly masters with respect and eagerness, with sincerity of motive, as [though you were fulfilling an obligation] to Christ. 6Do so, not merely when someone is watching, as if you meant only to please men, but, like slaves of Christ, do God's will

---

*d*Cf. Titus 3:5; Rom. 10:8-10.   *c*Cf. Gen. 2:24 and context.
*a*Cf. Exod. 20:12; Deut. 5:16.   *b*Cf. Gen. 18:19; Deut. 6:1ff.; 8:3.

from the heart. [7]Render service with goodwill, as to the Lord, and not to men, [8]remembering that the Lord will pay back every person, whether he is a slave or a free man, for whatever good thing he does.

[9]And you masters, show the same consideration for your slaves, and stop threatening them. Never forget that their Master—who is also yours—is in heaven, and he shows no partiality.

[10]Finally, keep empowered by the Lord and by the strength of his might. [11]Put on the complete battle equipment which God provides, so that you may be able to stand against the subtle tactics of the devil. [12]For our struggle is not against mortal beings, but against the demonic powers, against superhuman authorities, against the world-despots of this darkness, against the wicked spirit-forces of the upper regions.

[13]Therefore, utilize the complete battle equipment which God provides, so that when the day of Christ comes you may be able to resist [the enemy] in face-to-face combat, and, having performed everything your duty requires, to emerge with victory.

[14]So stand firm, having tightened the belt of truth around your waist. Put on the breastplate which consists of righteousness. [15]Wear for shoes the readiness to declare the gospel of peace. [16]In every encounter take faith for your shield. With it you will be able to extinguish all the flaming missiles hurled by the evil one. [17]Let salvation be your helmet, and [take] the Spirit's sword, which is the word of God. [Put on the full equipment] with much prayer and supplication.

[18]Pray at all times in the Spirit, keeping alert about this with continued perseverance and entreaty for all the saints. [19]And [ask] on my behalf that I may have freedom of speech to make known boldly the mystery disclosed by the gospel, [20]for the sake of which I am an ambassador held by a chain. Pray that I may declare the message fearlessly as it is my duty to do.

[21]Now in order that you, as well as others, may know how I am and what I am doing, Tychicus,[c] the beloved brother and trustworthy servant in the Lord, will inform you fully. [22]I am sending him to you for this very purpose, that you may know how we are getting along, and that he may cheer your hearts.

[23]Peace to the brothers and love with faith, from God the Father and the Lord Jesus Christ. [24]May divine favor be with all who have undying love for our Lord Jesus Christ.

---

cCf. Col. 4:7.

PHILIPPIANS

Chapter 1

Paul and Timothy, servants of Christ Jesus, to all the saints in Christ Jesus who are at Philippi, with the congregational overseers and their assistants: 2Grace to you and peace from God our Father and the Lord Jesus Christ.

3I thank my God upon every remembrance of you. 4Always, in every prayer, I pray for all of you with joy, 5because of your participation in [promoting] the gospel from the first day [you heard it] until now. 6And I am fully confident of this, that he who began a good work in you will bring it to completion at the Day of Christ Jesus. 7I am justified in maintaining this [confidence] in all of you, because I hold you in my heart, and all of you are cosharers with me in God's grace, both in my imprisonment and in the defense and vindication of the gospel.

8Indeed, God is my witness, how I yearn for all of you, with the compassion motivated by Christ Jesus. 9And it is my prayer that your love may abound yet more and more, with increasing insight and perception, 10enabling you to distinguish between things that differ [and to approve whatever meets the standard of God's word[a]], that you may be pure and blameless [in preparation] for the Day of Christ, 11being filled with the fruit which righteousness yields through Jesus Christ to the honor and praise of God.

12Now, I want you to know, brothers, that what has happened to me has actually helped to spread the gospel. 13In fact, it has become known throughout the Praetorian Guard and elsewhere that I am in prison in [connection with the service of] Christ. 14And most of the brothers in the Lord, having had their confidence strengthened through my imprisonment, are showing more and more boldness in speaking God's word without fear.

15Some are preaching from motives of envy and strife, while others [do so] because of good will. 16Those who [preach him] out of love

---

aImplied by context.

know that I am appointed for the gospel's defense. [17]But the others are proclaiming Christ from rivalry, with impure motives, supposing that they are making my imprisonment more difficult to bear. [18]What does it matter? The main thing is that, regardless of the motive, Christ is preached, and in this I rejoice. Yes, and I shall continue rejoicing, [19]for I know that, through your prayers and the help supplied by the Spirit of Jesus Christ, the present state of things will result in my deliverance [20]in fulfillment of my eager expectation and hope that in nothing shall I ever be made ashamed, but that with complete boldness now as always Christ will be magnified in me, whether by my life or by my death.

[21]For to me, to live is Christ and to die is gain. [22]But if I keep on living in this mortal body, [I shall have the opportunity of gathering more] fruit from my labor. So I do not know which to prefer. [23]I am torn between the two. I have a longing to depart and be with Christ, which would be far better. [24]Yet to remain in the present life is more beneficial for you. [25]And since I am fully convinced of this, I am quite sure that I shall remain a while longer and continue with all of you for your progress and joy in the faith. [26]So, with regard to me, your rejoicing may abound in Christ Jesus when I visit you again.

[27]But whatever happens, conduct yourselves in a manner worthy of the gospel of Christ, so that whether I come and see you, or in my absence hear about what you are doing, [I may be assured] that you are standing firm in one spirit, and one purpose, striving side by side for the faith of the gospel. [28]Do not be frightened in any way by your adversaries. Your [fearlessness] is an indication of utter defeat for them, but of salvation for you—and that from God.

[29]For you have been granted the privilege not only of trusting in Christ, but also of suffering for him. [30]You are carrying on the same kind of struggle in which you saw me engaged[b] and in which, as you hear, I am still involved.

Chapter 2

Therefore, by whatever[a] persuasiveness there is in Christ, by whatever incentive there is in love, by whatever participation is prompted

---

[b]Cf. Acts 16:19ff.

[a]In this verse there are four grounds of appeal expressed by four first class conditional clauses. The Apostle assumes that his readers know the realities of Christian experience.

by the Spirit, by whatever deep affection and tenderness is yours, [2]make my joy complete by thinking harmoniously, reciprocating with purposive goodwill, and with oneness of soul, keeping one aim in view. [3]Do nothing through rivalry or from excessive ambition, but in humility let each person regard others as excelling himself. [4]Each of you should be concerned not only about your own interests, but also about the interests of others.

[5]Let your attitude be that of Christ Jesus. [6]Although from the beginning he had the nature of God, he did not consider his equality with God as something to be exploited for himself, [7]but laid it aside in the sense that he assumed the nature of a servant[b] when he became like men. And having been recognized in physical appearance as a man, [8]he humbled himself [still further] by becoming obedient even unto death: the death of the cross.

[9]This is why God has so highly exalted him and conferred upon him the Name which is above every name, [10]that in the Name of Jesus every knee in heaven and on earth and under the earth shall bend, [11]and every tongue shall fully acknowledge that JESUS CHRIST IS LORD, to the glory of God the Father.

[12]Therefore, my beloved, just as you have always been obedient, not as in my presence only, but now all the more in my absence, with reverence and seriousness work out to completion the salvation of yourselves. [13]For it is God who is at work within you [imparting] both the desire and the energy [which enable you to do] his good will. [14]Carry out all your responsibilities without grumbling and dissension, [15]so that you may become blameless and pure, unblemished children of God in the midst of a crooked and perverse people.

Shine brightly among them like luminaries in [this dark] world, continuing to hold out to them the word of life. [16]Then, on the Day of Christ, I can glory in the fact that I did not run [my course] in vain, or labor for nothing. [17]In fact, even if [my blood] is poured out as a libation[c] along with [my] sacrifice and service for your faith,

---

[b]Literally, *having taken* the form of a servant. The aorist participle, *labōn,* is epexegetic and shows what is meant by our Lord's condescension. Paul's emphasis is not upon what Christ gave up (heavenly glory), but upon what he took up (humanity) in order to become the Savior of the world.

[c]The libation, frequent in both Jewish and pagan worship, was a drink offering, usually a cup of wine poured out during the ritual of sacrifice. The Apostle will use this metaphor again when he knows his execution is actually drawing near. Cf. 2 Tim. 4:6.

I am glad and rejoice with you all. [18]And [with regard to] this very thing, I want you to be glad and rejoice with me.

[19]Now I hope in the Lord Jesus to send Timothy to you before long, so that I, too, may be cheered by receiving news about you. [20]For I have no one as well qualified as he, who would show such genuine concern about your well-being. [21]The [others] are all pursuing their own interests—not those of Christ Jesus. [22]But you know how [Timothy] has stood the test, that like a son with his father he has worked hard with me for [the promotion of] the gospel. [23]So I hope to send him immediately after I see how things turn out with me. [24]And I am confident in the Lord that I myself shall come to you soon.

[25]But I consider it necessary to send [back] to you [at once] Epaphroditus, my brother and fellow worker and fellow soldier, whom you commissioned to minister to my needs. [26]He has been longing for you all, and troubled because you heard about his illness. [27]And in fact he did become ill, and almost died. But God had mercy on him, and not only on him but also on me, to prevent me from having sorrow upon sorrow. [28]Therefore I am eager to send him, so that you may rejoice at seeing him again, and that my burdens may be made lighter [by your joy]. [29]So welcome him gladly in the Lord. And honor men like him, [30]because it was for Christ's cause that he came near death, risking his life to do for me what you were not here to do.

Chapter 3

Furthermore, my brothers, keep rejoicing in the Lord. I do not hesitate to repeat what I have already written to you, because re-emphasizing these things is not unpleasant for me, and it is a safeguard for you.

[2]Beware of the dogs, beware of the evil workers, beware of the mutilators! [3]Actually we are the [true] circumcision: we who worship by the Spirit of God, who make our boast in Christ Jesus and put no reliance on any kind of human status—[4]although I myself might do so. If anyone thinks he has grounds to rely on human status, I [have] far more: [5]I was circumcised on the eighth day [after my birth]. I

descended from the stock of Israel, through the tribe of Benjamin. I am a son of parents who retained the Hebrew language and customs. With regard to the Law, I was a Pharisee. 6As far as zeal was concerned, I was a persecutor of the church. Measured by the standard of legal righteousness, I was blameless.

7But such things, which used to be gains for me, I have come to regard as loss for the sake of Christ. 8Indeed, as a matter of fact, I actually count everything as loss compared with the supreme value of knowing Christ Jesus my Lord, for whom I have suffered the loss of all things, and consider them rubbish, in order to gain Christ 9and be found in him, not having righteousness of my own, dependent upon [the observance of] law, but that which is through trust in Christ—God's kind[a] of righteousness which is conditioned on faith. 10I want to know Christ—to experience the power demonstrated by his resurrection, to share in his sufferings, and realize more and more what it means to be like him in his death, 11in the hope that I may attain to the resurrection from the dead.

12I do not mean that I have already reached [my highest aims], or have already been made perfect. But I keep pressing onward to lay hold of [the purpose] for which Christ Jesus laid hold of me. 13Brothers, I do not consider that I yet have grasped [that purpose completely]. But one thing [I do]: forgetting the past and eagerly stretching forward to what lies ahead, 14I press on toward the goal, for the prize of God's high calling in Christ Jesus.

15Therefore, let those of us who are mature hold this attitude. If you are striving for any other goal, God will reveal this to you. 16Nevertheless, let us keep in line, [continuing] in the same direction in which we have come thus far.

17Brothers, together follow my example, and observe carefully those who live according to the pattern you have in us.[b] 18For there are many—of whom I have told you often, and now tell you again even with weeping—who are enemies of the cross of Christ. 19Their end is perdition. Their god is bodily appetites. They are even proud of their immoral practices. Their thoughts are habitually upon earthly things.

---

[a]Cf. Rom. 1:17.

[b]The plural pronoun here probably refers to Timothy and Epaphroditus (cf. 1:1; 2:19-30), and to other faithful believers well known to the Philippians (4:3).

20But our citizenship is in heaven, from which we await eagerly the [appearing of the] Savior, even the Lord Jesus Christ, 21who will transform our lowly earthly bodies and make them like the body which he has in [his heavenly] glory. [This transformation will be accomplished] by the exercise of the power with which he is able even to subdue all things to himself.

Chapter 4

So in view of this glorious hope, my beloved brothers, whom I long to see—you who are my joy and reward—as I have exhorted you, keep standing firm in the Lord, my beloved.

2I implore Euodia and I implore Syntyche to agree in the Lord. 3Yes, and I ask you, faithful Synzygos—true yokefellow, to help these women. For they have toiled with me to advance the gospel, together with Clement and the rest of my fellow workers whose names are in the Book of Life.

4Rejoice in the Lord always! Again I will say, Rejoice! 5Let your reasonableness be known to everyone. The Lord is near. 6Do not worry about anything, but in every circumstance by prayer and supplication with thankfulness keep making your needs known to God. 7And God's peace, which surpasses all [our] comprehension, will keep guard over your hearts and thoughts in Christ Jesus.

8Finally, brothers, whatever is true, whatever commands respect, whatever is just, whatever is pure, whatever is winsome, whatever is well-spoken, whatever has excellence or merits praise—give careful consideration to these things. 9And what you have learned and received and heard and seen in me, these things practice. And the God of peace will be with you.

10It makes me rejoice greatly in the Lord to know that your care for my well-being has now flourished again[a]—indeed [all along] you were thinking about me but you had no opportunity [to express your concern]. 11This is not to say that I have any complaint. For I have learned to reduce my needs to a minimum. 12I know how to get along when resources are low, and I know how to enjoy plenty. In various

---

[a]Paul thanks the Philippians for the gifts they sent to him by Epaphroditus (cf. 2:25; 4:18).

places and circumstances [my experiences] have made me familiar with fullness and with hunger, with abundance and with scarcity. [13]Through him who constantly empowers me, I have strength for anything [which I may encounter].

[14]Nevertheless, you did well to share in my hardship. [15]And you Philippians yourselves well know that from the time the gospel was first preached in your region,[b] when I departed from Macedonia,[c] you were the only church that shared with me in the matter of giving and receiving. [16]Even [while I was] at Thessalonica,[d] more than once you supplied my needs.

[17]However, my main interest is not in the contribution itself, but in the spiritual benefit which giving brings to you. [18]I have enough of everything—in fact more than I need. I am fully supplied since I received what you sent by Epaphroditus. [It is like] fragrant incense, an acceptable sacrifice, well-pleasing to God. [19]And my God [who has so adequately provided for me], will fully supply your every need, according to his riches in glory through Christ Jesus. [20]To our God and Father be the glory forever and ever! Amen.

[21]Greet every saint in Christ Jesus. The brothers who are with me send their greetings. [22]All the saints, especially those of Caesar's household, greet you.

[23]May the gracious favor of the Lord Jesus Christ be with your spirit.

[b]Cf. Acts 16:12ff.   [c]Cf. Acts 17:14.   [d]Cf. Acts 17:1-9.

COLOSSIANS

Chapter 1

Paul, an apostle of Christ Jesus by God's will, and Timothy our brother, 2to the saints and faithful brothers in Christ at Colossae: May gracious favor be yours, and peace, from God our Father.

3We always give thanks to God the Father of our Lord Jesus Christ, when we pray for you, 4because we have heard of your loyalty to Christ Jesus and of the sacrificial love you have toward all the saints 5on account of the hope treasured up for you in heaven. You have already heard [about this hope] through the message of truth disclosed by the gospel.

6And just as it is spreading across the whole world, producing fruit and increasing, it is doing likewise among you ever since the day you heard [it] and came to know the grace of God in truth, 7even as you learned [it] from Epaphras our beloved fellow-servant. He is a faithful minister of Christ on your behalf, 8and it is he who brought us news about the love which the Spirit has imparted to you.

9That is why, since the day we heard [this news], we have not ceased to pray for you, asking God to fill you with the deeper knowledge of his will in complete spiritual wisdom and understanding, 10so that you may walk in a manner approved by the Lord, pleasing [him] completely, bearing fruit in every good work and advancing in this deeper knowledge of God.

11We pray that you may be strengthened by his glorious might with all the power you need for perseverance and longsuffering in every circumstance, [enabling you] with joy 12to give thanks to the Father who has qualified you to receive your share of the inheritance which the saints have in the realm of light. 13He has delivered us out of the dominion of the darkness and transferred us into the kingdom of his beloved Son, 14in whom we have redemption, the forgiveness of our sins.

[15]He is the exact likeness [and manifestation] of the invisible God. He is prior to and supreme over[a] all creation, [16]because through him were created all things in the heavens and upon the earth, things visible and invisible, whether thrones, lordships, rulers, or authorities. They were all created through him and for him.

[17]He himself existed before all things, and in him all things maintain their coherence. [18]He himself is the head of the body [of believers, which is] the church. He is the Primary Source,[b] the Ideal Representative [as the first to rise glorified[c]] from the dead, in order that he himself might be preeminent in every respect. [19]For it pleased [God] that all the characteristics of deity should dwell in him, [20]and through him [God chose] to reconcile all things to himself, whether things on the earth or things in the heavens—through him he made peace by the blood of his cross.

[21]So you, who were at one time in a state of estrangement, and hostile in attitude on account of your evil deeds, [22]he has now reconciled in the human body of Jesus, by means of his death, in order to present you holy and unblemished and irreproachable before him, [23]if indeed you continue in the faith, well grounded and steadfast, never deviating from the hope based on the gospel which you have heard, which has been preached in the whole creation under heaven, and of which I, Paul, have been appointed a minister.

[24]Now I rejoice in my sufferings on your behalf, and in my body I am filling up in due turn [my portion of] what Christ left us to endure[d] for the sake of his body, which is the church, [25]of which I have been made a servant by God's appointment, given to me for your benefit, to set forth the word of God in its fulness, [26]the secret purpose, hidden during past ages and generations but now made plain to his saints.

[27]To them God chose to make known among the Gentiles how rich is the glory of this revealed secret, which is Christ in you, the hope of glory, [28]whom we proclaim, admonishing every man and teaching every man in all [essential] wisdom, that we may present every man complete in Christ. [29]For this purpose I toil, struggling according to his sustaining power which is working mightily in me.

---

[a]In this context the Greek compound adjective, *prōtotokos*, seems to express both priority and supremacy.
[b]Or, the Beginning.
[c]Cf. Rom. 8:29; 1 Cor. 15:20; 23; Phil. 3:21.
[d]Cf. 2 Cor. 1:5; 4:10; 1 Thess. 3:3.

Chapter 2

I want you to know what great concern I have for you, and for those at Laodicea, and for all who have not seen me face to face, ²that their hearts may be strengthened, being knit together in divine love, and [that they may become aware of] all the wealth of the full assurance which understanding imparts. Thus they may reach the thorough knowledge of God's revealed secret, which is Christ, ³in whom are all the hidden treasures of wisdom and knowledge. ⁴I say this to prevent anyone from leading you astray by deceitful speech. ⁵Although I am absent in body, yet I am present in spirit, rejoicing at seeing your unbroken ranks and the integrity of your faith in Christ.

⁶Just as you received Christ Jesus the Lord, live in vital relationship with him, ⁷being firmly settled and built up in him, growing stronger in the faith, as you have been taught it,ᵃ abounding in thanksgiving.

⁸See that no one takes you captive by means of the philosophy characterized by vain deceit—that which follows human tradition and the elementary things of the world instead of Christ. ⁹For in him the full measure of the very essence of God abides in bodily form, ¹⁰and you have been brought to a state of completeness in him, who is the Head of all rule and authority.

¹¹And in relation to him you were circumcised, not by a rite performed by human hands, but by the spiritual circumcision wrought by Christ in liberating you from [the domination of] the old nature. ¹²With him you were buried in baptism,ᵇ and with him you were also raised up through trust in the mighty action of God, who raised him from the dead.

¹³So you—who were spiritually dead due to the misdeeds and the uncircumcision of your old nature—you he made alive together with Christ, when he graciously forgave all ourᶜ misdeeds. ¹⁴He cancelled the document of indebtedness, which by means of its decrees had a claim upon us. And he removed it permanently by nailing it to the cross. ¹⁵He disarmed the [antagonistic] powers and authorities, ex-

---

ᵃCf. 1:7.   ᵇCf. Rom. 6:3-4.

ᶜThe change from the second to the first person indicates Paul's eagerness to declare his own experience of God's forgiveness.

posing them openly [as defeated foes] when he triumphed over them by means of the cross.

16Therefore, stop allowing anyone to criticize you in matters of eating and drinking, or with regard to a festival or a new moon or a sabbath. 17These were only a shadow of things to come, but the reality [they typified] belongs to Christ. 18Let no one defraud you of your prize, even if he seeks to do so by an air of humility and by advocating the mediation of angels, acting as if he has special insight into unseen things. Such a man is puffed up by the futile speculations of his unregenerate nature. 19He is not maintaining union with him who is the Head, from whom the entire body, nourished and held together by means of its contacts and bonds, grows as it receives energy from God.

20If through union with Christ you died to the crude notions of the world, why, as though you still belonged to the world, do you allow yourselves to be subjected to decrees [such as], 21"Do not handle this! Do not taste that! Do not touch those!" 22—references to things which cease to exist as soon as they are used? Rules of that kind are only man-made injunctions and precepts. 23Such regulations make a pretense of wisdom by advocating self-imposed worship and so-called humility and austere asceticism, [but are] worthless in combatting the desires of the unregenerate nature.

Chapter 3

So if you have been raised up with Christ, keep seeking the things that are above, where Christ is, seated at God's right hand. 2Keep thinking about heavenly things, not about earthly things. 3For you died [in your identification with his death], and your life [which is the result of his resurrection], is hidden with Christ in God. 4When Christ, who is our life, is manifested [in his ultimate splendor], then you too will be manifested with him in glory.

5Therefore, put to death completely and at once all those practices which would make your bodily faculties the instruments of sin—fornication, impurity, sensual cravings, evil longings, and covetousness, for that is idolatry. 6It is because of these very sins that God's indignation comes. [7]You used to participate in such vices when you walked in the sphere of sin. [8]But now you must cast them all aside—wrath, anger, ill-will, blasphemy, and abusive speech.

[9]Make it a rule not to lie to one another. Put off completely the old man with his deeds, [10]and put on the new man who is continually being renewed through deeper knowledge in conformity with the likeness of his Creator. [11]In this new life there does not exist Greek and Jew, circumcision and uncircumcision, barbarian, Scythian, slave, free man—but Christ is everything and he is in us all.

[12]As God's chosen and holy people, who are the recipients of his love, clothe yourselves with tender compassion, kindness, humility, meekness, longsuffering. [13]Bear with one another, and graciously forgive each other if there is a complaint against anyone. Just as the Lord has graciously forgiven you, so you too [must forgive others]. [14]And above all these qualities, put on love, which is the bond of completeness. [15]And let the peace that Christ gives, to which you were called into one body, control your hearts. And always be thankful.

[16]Let the word of Christ dwell in you with its wealth of meaning, enabling you to teach and admonish yourselves in all [essential] wisdom. With psalms and hymns and spiritual songs, sing with gratitude in your hearts to God. [17]And whatever you do and whatever you say, do everything and say everything in the name of the Lord Jesus, giving thanks to God the Father through him.

[18]Wives, be submissive to your husbands, as is proper in the Lord. [19]Husbands, treat your wives with the highest affection. Always be considerate toward them. [20]Children, obey your parents in all respects, for this is well-pleasing to the Lord. [21]Fathers, do not irritate your children, or they will become depressed. [22]Slaves, give your earthly masters full obedience, not merely with service that can be seen, as if you meant only to please men, but with sincerity of purpose based on your reverence for the Lord. [23]Whatever you do, work enthusiastically—as for the Lord and not for men. [24]For you know that from the Lord you will receive in turn the reward which consists of the inheritance. Keep serving the Lord Christ. [25]Indeed, whoever does wrong will be paid back for his wrongdoing. And [with God] there is no partiality.

Chapter 4

You who are masters, treat your slaves justly and fairly, realizing that you yourselves have a Master in heaven.

2Continue steadfastly in prayer. Keep alert as you pray, and be thankful. 3Pray in our behalf too, that God may open to us a door for the word, so that we may declare the revealed secret concerning Christ, on account of which I am kept in custody.

4Pray that I may proclaim the message clearly, just as it is my duty to do. 5Conduct yourselves wisely before outsiders. Make the best possible use of your time. 6Let your speech always be attractive, characterized by wholesomeness, that you may know how to reply in the most appropriate way to each individual.

7My beloved brother Tychicus, a faithful minister and a fellow servant in the Lord, will tell you about my circumstances. 8I am sending him to you for this very purpose, that you may learn how things are with us, and that he may encourage your hearts. 9Accompanying him will be Onesimus, the faithful and beloved brother, who is one of yourselves. They will inform you of everything that has happened here.

10Aristarchus, my fellow prisoner, greets you. So does Mark, Barnabas' cousin—about whom you have received instructions. If he comes to you, make him welcome—11and Jesus who is surnamed Justus. These are the only converts from Judaism serving as my co-workers [here] for the kingdom of God. They have been a great comfort to me.

12Epaphras, one of yourselves, greets you. He is a servant of Christ Jesus, [and] is continually wrestling in prayer on your behalf, that you may stand complete and fully assured in everything regarding God's will. 13Indeed, I can testify to the deep concern he has for you and for those at Laodicea and Hierapolis. 14Luke, the beloved physician, greets you, and so does Demas.

15Extend our greetings to the brothers in Laodicea, and to Nympha and the church that meets at her house. 16When this letter has been read among you, have it read also in the church of the Laodiceans. And see that you also read the letter [that should reach you] from Laodicea. 17And say to Archippus, "Take heed to the ministry which you have received in the Lord. Make sure that you carry out all the duties assigned to you."

18I, Paul, write this salutation with my own hand. Remember my bonds. May grace be with you.

FIRST THESSALONIANS

Chapter 1

Paul and Silvanus ^aand Timothy to the church of the Thessalonians in God the Father and in the Lord Jesus Christ: May divine favor be yours, and peace!

2We are constantly giving thanks to God for all of you, making mention of you each time we pray, 3remembering without ceasing your activity prompted by genuine faith, your toil motivated by love, and your perseverance sustained by the hope which you have in our Lord Jesus Christ before God our Father. 4We have come to know, brothers beloved by God, of his choice of you, 5from the fact that our gospel was not presented to you with words only, but also in [its characteristic] power, and with the Holy Spirit, and with much conviction—indeed you know what kind [of men] we demonstrated ourselves to be among you for your benefit—6and [from the fact that] you not only patterned your lives after us, but after the Lord, having welcomed the word [although it involved you] in much oppression, together with joy inspired by the Holy Spirit.

7Thus you became a pattern to all the believers in Macedonia and in Achaia. 8For from you the word of the Lord has sounded forth [and continues to be heard like a series of echoes] not only in Macedonia and Achaia, but [the report of] your faith toward God has gone out [with abiding results] everywhere, so that there is no need for us to mention it to anyone.

9For the people in various places are telling [openly and properly] of the kind of welcome you gave us, and how you turned away from your idols to the [only real] God, to serve the living and true God, 10 and to await [the return] from heaven of his Son, whom he raised from the dead, [even] Jesus who is our Deliverer from the coming wrath.

_aThe Silas of the Book of Acts. Silas was his Hebrew name and Silvanus his Roman name.

Chapter 2

Now you yourselves know, brothers, that our visit to you has not proved to be in vain. ²Although we had previously undergone suffering and shameful treatment at Philippi,ᵃ as you recall, we were bold in our God to speak to you the gospel of God amid a great deal of opposition.ᵇ ³Indeed, our appeal does not proceed from error, nor from impure motives,ᶜ nor is it based on deception. ⁴But just as we have been approved by God to be entrusted with the gospel, so we speak not to please men but [to please] God who tests our hearts.

⁵Actually we never once appeared before you with flattering speech, as you well know, nor with a covetous motive (God is our witness). ⁶Nor did we seek glory from men, either from you or from others. ⁷Although, as Christ's apostles, we had the right to make heavy demands, nevertheless we were gentle in your midst, like a nurse tenderly caring for her own children.

⁸Because of our deep affection for you, we were glad to impart to you not only the gospel of God but also our very lives because you had become so preciousᵈ to us. ⁹Certainly you remember, brothers, our fatiguing toil and difficult labor, [how we] worked by night and by day [to earn our living] in order not to place a burden upon any of you [when] we proclaimed to you the gospel of God. ¹⁰ You [are] witnesses, and [so is] God, of the holy and righteous and blameless manner in which we acted toward you who are believers. ¹¹You know how we treated each one of you like a father treats his own children, ¹²urging you and encouraging and appealing [to you]ᵉ to walk in a manner pleasing to God who calls you into his own kingdom and glory.

¹³Furthermore we are giving thanks unceasingly to God because when you received the word of God which you heard from us, you welcomed it not as man's word but as it truly is [in its very nature]: God's word—which in fact is at work in you who believe. ¹⁴Indeed, brothers, you have followed the example of the churches of God in Christ Jesus, which are in Judea, for you yourselves also suf-

---

ᵃCf. Acts 16:19-24, 37-39.　　　ᵇLiterally, *in much agony.*
ᶜLiterally, *from uncleanness.*
ᵈRendering verbal adjective of *agapaō*, which means to love with a concern that recognizes the value of the object loved.
ᵉOr, urging you, both by encouragement and by testimony.

fered the same things [at the hands of] your own countrymen as [those churches] did [at the hands of] the Jews, [15]who killed both the Lord Jesus and the prophets and drove us forth [from place to place[f]]. [The heedless Jews are] displeasing to God, and are enemies of all mankind, [16]because they are trying to prevent us from taking the message of salvation to the Gentiles. As a result [of their action, such Jews] always heap up the measure of their sins. Consequently [God's] wrath has come upon them completely.

[17]But we, brothers, having been painfully separated from you for a period of time, in bodily presence but not in heart, were exceedingly eager with ardent longing to see your faces. [18]We strongly desired to come to you—I, Paul, tried more than once—but Satan cut in to hinder us. [19]For what is our hope or joy or crown of boasting in the presence of the Lord Jesus at his coming? You are, are you not? [20]Yes, indeed! You are our glory and joy!

Chapter 3

Therefore when we could no longer endure [not hearing from you], we decided that it was best for me to be left in Athens alone, [2]so we sent Timothy, our brother and God's servant in the gospel of Christ, to strengthen and encourage you with reference to your faith, [3]so that none of you at any time should allow himself to be disturbed by these hardships. Certainly you yourselves know that our calling involves us in difficult circumstances. [4]For even when we were with you we used to tell you beforehand that we were about to undergo hardships; and sure enough it has come to pass, as you are well aware. [5]So, when I could not bear the suspense any longer, I sent [Timothy[a]] to find out about your faith, for I was afraid that the tempter might have enticed you and that possibly our labor had turned out to be in vain.

[6]But now Timothy has returned to us from [his visit with] you, and has brought us good news of your fidelity and love, and [has informed us] that you always have kind thoughts of us, and are as eager to see us as we are to see you. [7]For this reason, that is, through your faithfulness, brothers, we have been encouraged about you in

---

/Cf. Acts 17:5-15.   [a]Indicated by vv. 2 and 6.

spite of all our distress and hardship; [8]for it makes life worthwhile
for us if you continue standing firm in the Lord. [9]Indeed, how can
we give back to God adequate thanks for you, for all the joy with
which we rejoice because of you before our God, [10]while by night
and by day we are praying with exceeding earnestness that we may
see your faces and supply the things that are lacking in your faith.

[11]Now may God our Father himself, and our Lord Jesus, direct
our way to you; [12]and may the Lord cause you to increase and
abound in purposive concern for one another and for all men, even
as we [abound in this deep concern] for you. [13]May he establish your
hearts in holiness, so that you may be blameless in the sight of God
our Father at the appearing of our Lord Jesus with all his saints.

Chapter 4

With regard to what remains to be said, brothers, we request and
urge you in the Lord Jesus, that just as you have learned from us
how it is necessary for you to live and to please God—as indeed you
are doing—that you continue making progress. [2]For you know what
instructions we gave you by the authority of the Lord Jesus. [3]Indeed,
this is God's will [even] your sanctification: in [particular] that you
keep yourselves away from every kind of sexual vice; [4]that each one
of you may be able to acquire a wife for himself in sanctification and
honor, [5]not in lustful passion like the heathen who are in a state of
ignorance regarding God; [6]to prevent [any one of you] from trans-
gressing and taking advantage of his brother in this matter. For the
Lord is the avenger of all these things, as indeed we told you previously [when we] solemnly warned you [against such conduct].
[7]Certainly God has not called us for uncleanness, but [to live] in the
sphere of holiness. [8]Therefore whoever rejects [these admonitions]
rejects not man but God, who indeed imparts his Holy Spirit unto
you.

[9]Now concerning brotherly love, you have no need [for us] to
write to you, for you yourselves are God-taught to continue demonstrating purposive good will[a] to one another. [10]And in fact you are

---

[a]Present infinitive of the verb *agapaō*, which expresses the self-giving love revealed in
Christ.

practicing this toward all the brothers throughout Macedonia. [11]Yet we urge you, brothers, to continue making progress, and to use your utmost efforts to maintain an attitude of calmness, and to perform your personal duties, and to engage in meaningful work, as we instructed you, [12]so that your conduct will merit the confidence[b] of the outsiders and [that] you may earn your own support.[c]

[13]Now we do not want you to be without understanding, brothers, concerning those who from time to time fall asleep. We do not want you to go on being grieved as do others who have no hope. [14]For since we do believe that Jesus died and arose, thus also [we should believe that] God, by means of [this same] Jesus, will bring along with him the faithful who have fallen asleep. [15]For this we say to you by the word of the Lord, that we who are living, who survive until the coming of the Lord, will have no advantage whatsoever over those who have fallen asleep.

[16]For the Lord himself will come down from heaven with a loud summons, with the voice of an archangel, and with the trumpet blast of God, and the dead in Christ will rise first. [17]Then immediately we who are living, who survive, will be snatched up together with them, in [the] clouds, to meet the Lord in the air. And in this manner we shall be with the Lord forever. [18]Therefore, encourage one another with this assurance.[d]

Chapter 5

Now concerning the time periods and definite dates, brothers, you have no need [for anything] to be written to you, [2]for you yourselves know perfectly well that the Day of the Lord is coming in the manner in which a thief in the night comes. [3]When people[a] are saying, "Peace and security," then sudden ruin will come upon them, like birth pains upon an expectant mother, and there will be no possible means of escape. [4]But you, brothers, are not in darkness, so the Day [of the Lord] should not catch you by surprise.[b] [5]For all of you are sons of [the] light and sons of [the] day. We are not of [the character of] night or of darkness.

---

[b]Literally, *walk in a becoming manner.*   [c]Literally, *may have need of nothing.*
[d]Literally, *with these words.*
[a]Literally, *when they are saying.*   [b]Literally, *in the manner of a thief.*

⁶Accordingly, therefore, let us not be sleeping like the rest [of mankind,], but let us constantly be on the alert and maintain self-control. ⁷For those who sleep are sleeping at night, and those who yield themselves to drunkenness are drunk at night.

⁸But let us who are of [the character of] day maintain self-control, having put on the breastplate which consists of faith and divine love, and the headpiece which consists of the hope of salvation. ⁹For God has not appointed us for [the purpose of incurring] wrath, but for [the purpose of] obtaining salvation through our Lord Jesus Christ, ¹⁰who died in our behalf so that whether we live or die*c* we might have life with him. ¹¹So continue encouraging one another and edifying each other*d* just as you are doing.

¹²Now we request you, brothers, to appreciate those who are toiling among you, and leading*e* you in the Lord, and training*f* you. ¹³Esteem them very highly in love because of their work. Always be at peace among yourselves. ¹⁴And we exhort you, brothers, to admonish them that are out of line,*g* encourage the timid, hold on to the weak, show a great deal of patience toward everyone. ¹⁵See that no one [at any time] pays back evil for evil to anyone, but always seek the [highest] good for one another and for all men. ¹⁶Be joyful at all times. ¹⁷Never let up in your prayer life. ¹⁸Maintain an attitude of thankfulness regardless of circumstances. For this is God's will in Christ Jesus for you. ¹⁹Never quench the [fire of the] Spirit. ²⁰Never treat prophetic truths with contempt. ²¹But keep putting everything to the test, and continue holding fast to the good. ²²Always abstain from every kind of evil.

²³Now may the God of peace himself sanctify each of you entirely, and, [thus] complete in every aspect of your being, may your spirit and soul and body be kept [so as to be] blameless at the coming of our Lord Jesus Christ. ²⁴He who calls you is faithful, and he will do this.

²⁵Brothers, keep praying for us. ²⁶Greet all the brothers with a holy kiss. ²⁷I charge you by the Lord to have this epistle read to the entire congregation. ²⁸The gracious care of our Lord Jesus Christ be with you!

---

*c*Literally, *whether we are watching or sleeping.* A different application of two metaphors from v. 6. *d*Literally, *one the one.*

*e*Or, those who preside. Literally, *the ones who stand in front.* *f* Or, admonishing.

*g*The Greek substantive, *ataktous,* which means literally, *those who are out of line,* is used in the papyri of the Greco-Roman period to denote *idlers.*

SECOND THESSALONIANS

Chapter 1

Paul and Silvanus and Timothy to the church of the Thessalonians in God our Father and [in] the Lord Jesus Christ: 2May divine favor be yours, and peace from God the Father and the Lord Jesus Christ!

3We must continue giving thanks to God always for you, brothers, as it is proper [that we should], because your faith is growing exceedingly and the love of every one of you for each other is increasing. 4Consequently we ourselves are boasting about you among the churches of God for your perseverance and faith in [spite of] all the persecutions and hardships which you are enduring. 5This is a clear indication of the righteous judgment of God, whose purpose is that you may be counted worthy of the kingdom of God, in behalf of which you are indeed suffering.

6Certainly God considers it a just thing to give back oppression to those who are oppressing you, 7and [to give] to you who are being oppressed rest, along with us, at the revelation of the Lord Jesus from heaven with his mighty angels 8in flaming fire. He will give full vengeance to those who do not know God and to those who are not obeying the gospel of our Lord Jesus. 9Because of the character of such persons, they will pay the penalty which consists of eternal ruin away from the face of the Lord and from the glory of his might, 10when on that Day he comes to be glorified in his saints and to be admired by all those who have put their trust [in him]. [You will be included], because you believed the testimony we gave to you.

11To this end indeed we always pray for you that our God may count you worthy of this calling, and may fulfill [your] every desire for goodness and [every] endeavor of faith with power, 12in order that the name of our Lord Jesus may be glorified in you, and you in him, according to the gracious favor of our God and the Lord Jesus Christ.

Chapter 2

Now we request you, brothers, with regard to the coming of our Lord Jesus Christ and our being gathered together to meet him, [2]not to be easily shaken from your composure nor to go on being disturbed by any manner of spirit utterance, by any sort of oral statement, or by any kind of letter alleging to be from us, claiming that the Day of the Lord has arrived.[a] [3]Do not allow anyone to deceive you in any way whatsoever. For [the Day of the Lord will not come] unless the apostasy comes first, and there be revealed the man of lawlessness,[b] the son of perdition, [4]the one who opposes and exalts himself against everything which is called God or is an object of worship, so that he seats himself in the temple of God, proclaiming that he himself is God.

[5]You remember, do you not, that while I was yet with you I used to tell you these things? [6]So you know what is now[c] restraining him so that he may be revealed in his time. [7]For the latent principle of this lawlessness is already at work; only [the apostasy will not come and the man of lawlessness will not be revealed[d]] until he who is now exercising restraint gets out of the way. [8]And then will be revealed the lawless one, whom the Lord Jesus will slay by the breath of his mouth and will destroy by the manifestation of his parousia.

[9]The parousia of [the lawless one] is according to Satan's working, attended by all sorts of power and signs and wonders produced by falsehood, [10]and by every kind of deception which unrighteousness exerts on those who are perishing, because they did not receive the love of the truth by which they could have been saved. [11]Consequently God sends to them an influence characterized by error so that they believe the lie, [12]so that all who have not believed in the truth but have delighted in the unrighteousness may receive judgment.

[13]Now we on our part are obligated to give thanks always to God for you, brothers having been loved by the Lord [and abiding in the results of his love], because from the beginning[e] God chose you

---

[a]Rendering *enestēken*, the perfect tense of *enistēmi, to be present.* (Cf. cognate perfect participles which denote *things present:* Rom. 8:38; 1 Cor. 3:22; 7:26; Gal. 1:4; Heb. 9:9).
[b]Some manuscripts read, *the man of sin.*
[c]Or, now you know what is restraining [him].
[d]Filling in the hiatus as implied by context, especially by v. 3b.
[e]Rendering *ap' archēs.* Some manuscripts read, *aparchēn, firstfruits.*

for salvation through sanctification wrought by the Spirit and by faith in the truth. [14]It was to this end that he called you by means of our gospel, so that you may obtain [a share in] the glory of our Lord Jesus Christ. [15]In the light of these things, brothers, keep stand·ing firm, and maintain a strong grip on the truths which you were taught by us, whether by word of mouth or by letter.

[16]Now may our Lord Jesus Christ himself, and God our Father, who loved us and gave[f] us inexhaustible encouragement and reliable hope on the basis of his grace, [17]encourage and establish your hearts in every good work and word.

Chapter 3

Finally, brothers, keep praying for us, that the word of the Lord may continue to spread rapidly and accomplish its purpose even as [it is doing] with you, [2]and that we may be delivered from the troublesome and wicked men; for not everyone has faith. [3]But the Lord is faithful. He will establish and guard you from the evil one. [4]And we are persuaded in the Lord with regard to you, that you are doing and will continue to do the things which we are commanding. [5]Moreover, may the Lord open your hearts into [a deeper realization of] the love of God[a] and the perseverance shown by Christ.

[6]Now we command you, brothers, in the name of the Lord Jesus Christ, to withdraw yourselves from every brother whose conduct is disorderly[b] and not in accord with the truth[c] which you received from us. [7]Indeed you yourselves know how you ought to pattern your lives after us, for we were not idle among you. [8]We did not eat bread as a free gift from anyone, but by toil and exertion it was our practice to work by night and by day in order not to place a

---

[f]The singular aorist participles, *loved* and *gave*, may refer to the Father only, but it is grammatically possible that they refer also to the Lord Jesus Christ. The latter force would indicate the equality and the unity of action of the two divine persons. (Cf. 1 Thess. 3:11, where *kateuthunai, may he direct*, the third person singular aorist optative, makes Jesus the co-subject with God the Father.)

[a]The genitive may be subjective (God's love for us), or objective (our love for God). Actually, both ideas seem to be included.

[b]Literally, *out of line*. See footnote on 1 Thess. 5:14.

[c]Greek, *paradosis, tradition*. Literally, *that which is handed over*. Used by Paul of the definite body of Christian doctrine which was to be carefully preserved and transmitted. Cf. the plural in 2 Thess. 2:15; 1 Cor. 11:2.

burden upon any of you. [9][We did so] not because we lack the right [to receive support], but that we might give ourselves as a pattern for you to follow. [10]For even when we were with you, we used to emphasize this principle: If anyone is not willing to work, he shall not eat! [11]Now we are hearing about some among you who are wasting their time in idleness, doing nothing constructive, but interfering with the work of others.

[12]By the [authority of] the Lord Jesus Christ we command and exhort such persons to work without disturbance [and] earn their own living. [13]And as for you, brothers, never once lose heart in well-doing.

[14]Now if anyone does not obey our word [expressed] by this epistle, take note of that man—do not associate intimately with him[d] —in order that he may feel ashamed. [15]Do not regard him as an enemy, but keep admonishing him as a brother.

[16]Now may the Lord of peace himself give you his peace at all times in all circumstances. The Lord be with you all. [17]This greeting is in my own handwriting, which is a token of genuineness in every letter of mine. This is the manner in which I write—Paul. [18]The gracious care of our Lord Jesus Christ be with you all!

---

[d]Literally, *do not be mixed up together with him.*

FIRST TIMOTHY

Chapter 1

Paul, an apostle of Christ Jesus by command of God our Savior and Christ Jesus our Hope, 2to Timothy my genuine son[a] in the faith: Gracious favor, mercy, [and] peace [to you] from God our Father and Christ Jesus our Lord!

3As I urged you when I was departing for Macedonia, stay on at Ephesus in order that you may warn certain individuals to cease teaching erroneous doctrines, 4and to stop paying attention to endless fables and genealogies. For such things induce speculations rather than promoting our God-given responsibility which is performed through faith.

5Now the purpose of the warning [which you are to give] is love that flows from a pure heart, a clear conscience, and a sincere loyalty. 6By deviating from these qualities, some persons have missed the mark and have turned aside to worthless discussion. 7They want to be teachers of the Law, but they understand neither the terms they use nor the subject matter about which they speak so confidently.

8Now we are aware that the Law is excellent if anyone uses it properly, 9keeping in mind that law is not enacted for the righteous, but for the lawless and unruly, the impious and sinful, the unholy and profane, for those who strike their own fathers and mothers, for murderers, 10fornicators, homosexuals,[b] slave dealers,[c] liars, those who speak falsely under oath, and for [those guilty of] any other kind of behavior contrary to the sound teaching 11set forth in the gospel of the glory of the blessed God, with which I have been entrusted.

12I am thankful to Christ Jesus our Lord, who has given me adequate strength, that he considered me trustworthy and put me into

aGreek, *teknon, child.* Used frequently by Paul as a term of endearment. Cf. 1:18; 2 Tim. 1:2; 2:1; Titus 1:4; Philemon 10.
bCf. Lev. 18:22; 20:13; Deut. 23:17; Rom. 1:27.　　cCf. Exod. 21:16; Deut. 24:7.

this ministry, [13]even though previously I was a blasphemer and a persecutor and an atrocious man. But I was treated with mercy because, being ignorant, I had acted in unbelief. [14]Indeed, the grace of our Lord was showered [upon me] in great abundance, along with the faith and love which are realized through union with Christ Jesus.

[15]It is a true saying, and worthy of complete acceptance: "Christ Jesus came into the world to save sinners." Of these I myself am the foremost. [16]But I received mercy for a special purpose that, in me as the foremost sinner, Jesus Christ might display the full extent of his longsuffering as an object lesson for those who would later receive eternal life by believing on him. [17]Now to the King of the ages, the imperishable, invisible, and only God, be honor and glory for ever and ever! Amen.

[18]This charge[d] I commit to you, Timothy my son, in accordance with the prophecies previously given to you,[e] in order that by means of them you may wage the good warfare, [19]maintaining faith[f] and a good conscience. Some, by thrusting aside [the warnings of conscience], have made shipwreck of their faith. [20]Among these are Hymenaeus and Alexander, whom I have handed over to Satan.[g] Such discipline may teach them not to blaspheme.

Chapter 2

Now, as a matter of first importance, I urge that supplications, prayers, intercessions, and thanksgivings be made in behalf of everyone, [2]especially for rulers and all who occupy positions of eminence, so that we may lead quiet and peaceable lives with complete godliness and the seriousness which commands respect. [3]This is excellent and acceptable before God our Savior, [4]who desires everyone to be saved and to come to full knowledge of the truth.

[5]Indeed, there is one God, and one Mediator between God and men: the Man Christ Jesus, [6]who gave himself as a substitutionary sacrifice in behalf of all men. Testimony [has been given to this fact] at the proper times, [7]and for the purpose of proclaiming this testimony I myself was appointed a herald and an apostle—I am speak-

---

[d]Cf. 1:3, 5. [e]Or, the prophecies previously expressed about you. Cf. Acts 16:2.
[f]Or, faithfulness. [g]Cf. 1 Cor. 5:5.

ing the truth, I am not dealing in falsehood—a teacher of the Gentiles in the realm of faith and truth.

⁸Therefore I desire that the men pray in every place, lifting up holy hands, with no anger or ill will.ᵃ ⁹In a similar attitude, women should dress with modesty and discretion, not adorning themselves by braiding their hair,ᵇ or by wearing gold or pearls or expensive attire, ¹⁰but, as is proper for women who claim to be God-fearing, by means of good deeds.

¹¹Let a woman learn in quietness, in all submissiveness. ¹²I do not permit a woman to teach to the extentᶜ of exercising authority over a man, but to abide in quietness. ¹³From the fact that Adam was created first, and Eve afterwards [we see God's design for the headshipᵈ of the man]. ¹⁴Furthermore, Adam was not seduced [by the tempterᵉ], but the woman was completely seduced and was caught in transgression. ¹⁵However she will be saved through childbearing, if theyᶠ continue in faith and love and holiness along with discretion.

Chapter 3

It is a true saying: "If anyone aspires to the office of overseer [of a congregation], he sets his heart upon an excellent task." ²The overseer, then, must be unassailable in character, the husband of only one wife, clearheaded, balanced in judgment, well ordered [in his manner of life], hospitable, qualified to teach, ³not addicted to wine, not overbearing but gentle, not quarrelsome, not a lover of money.

⁴He must manage well his own household, maintaining the respect of his children with complete dignity on his part.ᵃ ⁵For if a man is

---

ᵃOr, doubting.

ᵇIn first-century Roman society, women of means decked themselves with glittering displays of costly ornaments. Hair dressing was done by special coiffeurs among the slaves. The hair braids were fastened by tortoiseshell combs inset with gems, or by pins of silver, bronze, or ivory. The jewelled pinheads consisted often of miniature images or idols of various kinds.

ᶜIndicated by the negative conjunction, *oude,* used here in an explanatory sense which clarifies the principle involved in the prohibition. Paul did not absolutely forbid women to teach. Cf. 1 Cor. 11:5.

ᵈThe man's headship involves his obligation to love and care for his wife. Cf. Eph. 5:22-23. ᵉCf. Gen. 3:4-6, 13.

ᶠBy changing from the singular to the plural, the Apostle's thought passes from woman generically as typified in Eve, to women in particular who exhibit the qualities of the Christian life. ᵃOr, on their part.

not able to manage his own household, how can he take care of a church of God? 6He should not be a spiritual novice, or he may get puffed up*b* [with conceit] and fall into the condemnation incurred by the devil. 7He must also have a good reputation among outsiders, or he may fall into reproach and [get caught in] a trap set by the devil.

8Deacons, likewise, must have a character that commands respect. They must not be inconsistent in what they say, not given to excess wine, not motivated by a desire for personal gain. 9They must hold fast to the revealed secret*c* of the faith with a pure conscience. 10They should first be tested for a reasonable time, after which, if no disqualifying charge is placed against them, let them be permitted to serve. 11Similarly, the women*d* must have a character that commands respect, not slanderers, clearheaded, faithful in all things. 12A deacon must have only one wife, and manage well his children and his own home. 13Indeed, those who serve efficiently acquire a good standing for themselves, and great boldness in proclaiming the faith which is centered in Christ Jesus.

14I hope to come to you soon, but I am writing these things to you 15so that if I am delayed you may know how people are required to conduct themselves*e* in God's household, which is the church of the living God, the custodian and citadel of the truth. 16There is no doubt about it, great is the revealed secret which finds expression in our religion:

> Christ*f* was manifested in human nature,
> He was vindicated in his spirit,*g*
> He was seen by angels,
> He was preached among the nations,
> He was believed on in the world,
> He was taken up in glory.

---

*b*Literally, *be-smoked,* or *wrapped in smoke.* The metaphor here suggests loss of spiritual vision due to the darkening effects of pride resulting from the rapid advancement of an immature person.

*c*Cf. note 1 Cor. 2:7.

*d*This reference may be to wives of deacons, but more probably it is to women deacons.

*e*Or, how you should conduct yourself.

*f*Some manuscripts read *theos, God.* Our text says *hos, who,* the masculine relative pronoun, and it clearly refers to Christ for he is certainly the subject of the six expressions which follow.

*g*Or, by the Spirit.

Chapter 4

But the Spirit says distinctly that in later times some persons will depart from the faith, devoting themselves to deceptive spirits and to doctrines that demons teach ²through the hypocrisy of liars whose consciences are so burned out[a] [that they have no feeling of right or wrong]. ³They will forbid marriage and insist on abstinence from certain foods—although God created these things[b] to be enjoyed with thanksgiving by those who are believers and have attained a full knowledge of the truth. ⁴Indeed, everything God created is good, and nothing need be rejected if it is received with gratitude. ⁵For it is sanctified[c] by the word of God and prayer.

⁶If you call the attention of the brothers to these principles, you will be an excellent minister of Christ Jesus, sustained by the precepts of the faith—even of the sound doctrine you have been following consistently. ⁷Never pay any attention to the valueless and imaginary tales which superstitious people tell.

Keep yourself in training with regard to godliness. ⁸Bodily exercise is of some benefit, but godliness is of supreme benefit because it provides assurance for the present life and for that which is to come. ⁹That saying is true and worthy of universal acceptance. ¹⁰This is why we toil and struggle, because we have retained[d] our hope in the living God, who is the Savior of all men, especially of believers.

¹¹Keep emphasizing and teaching these things. ¹²Let no one look down on you because you are young, but exemplify what a believer should be in speech, in behavior, in love, in faith,[e] in purity. ¹³Until I come, give close attention to the reading of the Scriptures,[f] to the exhortation,[g] [and] to the instruction.[h]

---

[a]Or, branded. Under Roman law criminals and runaway slaves were marked upon the forehead by a branding instrument of hot iron. In this verse the metaphor would refer to the mark of Satan upon the seared consciences of those enslaved by him.

[b]Literally, *which things God created.*

[c]Or, set apart for its divinely intended use.

[d]Implied by *ēlpikamen,* perfect active indicative, which expresses a continuing state of hope.

[e] Or, faithfulness.

[f]This may refer to public reading of Scripture, a feature of the synagogue rites (cf. Luke 4:16; Acts 15:21), which was adopted by the Christian congregations. Cf. 1 Thess. 5:21, 27; Col. 4:16; Rev. 1:3, 11.

[g]Cf. Acts 13:15.

[h]The use of the article with each of these three functions may indicate that they were well-known parts of the public worship.

[14]Do not fail to exercise your special gift, which was imparted to you through prophetic intimations about your work,[i] accompanied by the laying on of hands by the elders. [15]Always give careful consideration to these duties. Keep completely absorbed in them, so that your progress may be evident to everyone. [16]Keep a close check on yourself, and on the doctrine. Be faithful in these responsibilities, for by so doing you will save both yourself and those who listen to you.

Chapter 5

Never give a sharp rebuke to an older man, but appeal to him as if he were your father. Treat younger men as brothers, [2]older women as mothers, younger women as sisters, with purity of thought, speech, and actions.[a]

[3]Take care of widows who have no means of support.[b] [4]But if any widow has children or grandchildren, let these first learn their religious obligation to their own household and give back proper care to those who brought them up. For this is acceptable in the sight of God.

[5]Now a real widow—one who has been left all alone—has no hope but God, and continues in supplications and prayers by night and by day.[c] [6]But she who lives in self-indulgence is actually dead even while she is alive.

[7] Keep emphasizing these directives to them, so that they may be without reproach. [8]Whoever does not provide for his relatives, and especially for his own family, has denied the faith. He is worse than an unbeliever.

[9]To be placed on the list of widows, a woman must be at least sixty years of age. [She must have been] faithful to her husband. [10]She must have a good reputation as an excellent worker—one who has brought up children, shown hospitality, washed the feet of saints, given aid to people in distress, devoted herself to good deeds of every kind.

---

[i]Cf. footnote on 1 Tim. 1:18.   [a]Literally, *with all purity.*
[b]Literally, *Honor widows who really are widows.*
[c]*Night* and *day* are Greek nouns in the genitive case, hence specify the time, not the extent, of the prayers. Cf. 1 Thess. 3:10; 2 Tim. 1:3.

11But do not put younger women on the list of widows. For whenever the impulses of sexual desire become stronger than their dedication to Christ, they want to marry, 12and then are condemned for setting aside their first commitment. 13Furthermore, as they go about from house to house, they get the habit of idleness. Nor are they merely idle, but they also become nonsensical talkers and curiosity-seekers, saying things they should not.

14Therefore, I recommend that younger women*d* marry, bear children, manage their own households, giving the adversary no opportunity for slander. 15For already some have turned aside to follow Satan. 16If any woman believer has [relatives who are] widows, let her aid them, and let the church not be burdened [with their upkeep], so that it may aid those who are actually destitute.

17Let the elders who are excellent leaders be considered worthy of double honor,*e* especially those who work diligently at preaching and teaching. 18For the Scripture says, "You shall not muzzle the ox while it is treading out the grain,"*f* and, "The workman deserves his pay."*g* 19Do not receive an accusation against an elder, unless it is supported by two or three witnesses.*h* 20Those who habitually sin you are to reprove in the presence of all, so that the rest may be warned against wrongdoing.

21Before God and Christ Jesus and the select angels, I solemnly charge you to carry out these directives without prejudice, doing nothing on the basis of partiality. 22Make it a practice not to ordain*i* anyone hastily. Do not participate in the sins of others. Always keep yourself pure. 23Stop drinking only water, but use a little wine for the sake of your stomach and your frequent ailments.

24The sins of some men are clearly evident, preceding them to judgment, but [the sins] of others become known in due time. 25Similarly, excellent deeds are clearly evident. And even if they are not noticed readily, they cannot be hidden permanently.

*d*Doubtless Paul speaks directly to young widows, but his recommendation is not limited to them (cf. 1 Thess. 4:3-5; Titus 2:4-5).
*e*Or, double pay. Probably the Greek expression, *diplēs timēs*, includes both the idea of respect and that of adequate remuneration.
*f*Deut. 25:4.   *g*Luke 10:7; cf. Matt. 10:10.
*h*Cf. Deut. 19:15.
*i*Literally, *not to lay hands on.* Cf. 1 Tim 4:14; 2 Tim. 1:6.

Chapter 6

All who are under the yoke of slavery should consider their masters worthy of proper respect, so that the name of God and the doctrine may not be slandered. ²Slaves who have masters that are believers should not think lightly of them because they are their brothers, but should render even better service inasmuch as those who benefit by it are faithful and valued friends.

Constantly teach and urge these things. ³If anyone teaches doctrines of a different kind,[a] and does not consent to sound words—words given by our Lord Jesus Christ—even to the teaching which promotes godliness, ⁴he has become conceited,[b] having no real knowledge but a morbid desire for controversy and word battles, out of which arise envy, strife, denunciations, vile suspicions, ⁵and continuous friction between men whose minds have reached such a state of confusion that they are completely deprived of the truth, supposing that godliness is a means of gain. ⁶Godliness, accompanied by contentment,[c] is of course a means of great gain.

⁷[Material things have no permanent value], for we brought nothing into the world, and we cannot take anything out.[d] ⁸So if we have food and covering, with these we shall be content. ⁹But those who resolve to become rich fall into temptation and a snare and into many foolish and hurtful cravings which drag men down to ruin and perdition. ¹⁰Actually, evils of every kind spring from the love of money. In their eagerness to grasp wealth, some individuals have been led astray from the faith and have brought many sorrows upon themselves.

¹¹But you, O man of God, always shun such things. Concentrate on integrity, godliness, faith, love, endurance, gentleness. ¹²Keep up the good struggle for the faith. Get a firm grip on eternal life, to which you were called when you made the good confession in the presence of many witnesses.

¹³I charge you before God who gives life to all things, and before Christ Jesus who bore witness to the good confession in the time of[e]

---

[a]Literally, *If anyone teaches heterodoxy.* Cf. cognate infinitive in 1:3.
[b]Cf. 3:6.

[c]Or, competence. The Greek noun, *autarkeia,* in the Pauline sense, denotes the self-sufficiency which makes a person independent of earthly circumstances because his reliance is upon God. Cf. 2 Cor. 9:8.

[d]Cf. Job 1:21; Eccl. 5:15.　　　　[e]Indicated by preposition, *epi.*

Pontius Pilate, [14]to carry out your commission without stain and beyond reproach until the appearance of our Lord Jesus Christ, [15]which will be disclosed at the proper time by the blessed and only Sovereign, the King of kings and Lord of lords, [16]who alone is deathless, who dwells in unapproachable light, whom no man has seen or can see. To him be honor and dominion forever! Amen.

[17]As for those who are wealthy in the present age, charge them not to be haughty, nor to set their hope on uncertain riches but on God who richly provides us with all things for our enjoyment. [18]Instruct them to practice doing good, to be rich in noble deeds, to be quick to contribute, sympathetic in sharing with others, [19]treasuring for themselves a solid foundation for the future, so they may grasp the life that is really life.

[20]O Timothy, guard the deposit [of truth which has been entrusted to you]. Keep turning away from the futile, empty chatter and contradictions made by what is falsely called knowledge. [21]By professing it, some individuals have missed the mark concerning the faith.

May God's gracious favor be with all of you.

SECOND TIMOTHY

Chapter 1

Paul, an apostle of Christ Jesus, appointed through God's will to proclaim the promise of the life which is in Christ Jesus, 2to Timothy my dear son:[a] Gracious favor, mercy, and peace be yours from God the Father and Christ Jesus our Lord.

3I am thankful to God whom I serve—as did my forefathers—with a clear conscience, that unceasingly I make mention of you in my prayers by night and by day. 4I remember the tears you shed [when we parted], and I long to see you so that I may be filled with joy. 5I am reminded of the sincere faith which resided first in your grandmother Lois and in your mother Eunice and which, I am confident, is also in you.

6On the basis of this confidence I remind you to keep stirring the fire of the special gift you received from God when my hands were laid upon you. 7For God has not given us a spirit of timidity but [a spirit] of power and love and balanced judgment. 8So do not be ashamed of the testimony concerning our Lord, or of me his prisoner. But be a fellow sufferer for the gospel by the power of God, 9who has saved us and called [us] to consecrated service, not on the basis of our deeds but on the basis of his own purpose and gracious favor which was granted to us in Christ Jesus before time began,[b] 10and now has been clearly expressed through the appearance of our Savior Christ Jesus, who has rendered death ineffective [in all its aspects and consequences] and brought life and immortality to light by means of the gospel, 11for which I myself have been appointed a herald and an apostle and a teacher. 12That is the reason why I suffer as I do.

But I am not ashamed, for I know him whom I have trusted, and I stand persuaded that he is able to perpetuate until that Day the

---

aCf. 1 Tim. 1:2.
bCf. Titus 1:2.

deposit of truth which he committed to me.[c] [13]Keep holding to the pattern of sound words you have heard from me, in the faith and love that are centered in Christ Jesus. [14]By the aid of the Holy Spirit who dwells in us, guard[d] the excellent deposit [or truth committed to your care].

[15]You know that all those in [the province of] Asia have turned away from me,[e] including Phygelus and Hermogenes. [16]May the Lord show mercy to the household of Onesiphorus, because he often refreshed me and was not ashamed of my chain. [17]Indeed, when he came to Rome, he searched eagerly for me and found me. [18]May the Lord grant him to find mercy from the Lord on that Day! [19]And you know well the many services he rendered at Ephesus.

Chapter 2

So you, my son, continue being made strong by means of the grace derived from Christ Jesus. [2]And the instructions you heard from me in the presence of many witnesses, commit to reliable men who will be qualified to instruct others. [3]Endure your share of hardship as a good soldier of Christ Jesus. [4]A soldier does not entangle himself in the ordinary affairs of life, but his aim is to please his commander. [5]And no athlete can win the victor's crown unless he completes the contest according to the rules. [6]The hardworking farmer should be the first to share in the harvest. [7]Think about what I am saying, for the Lord will give you understanding in all these things.

[8]Remember Jesus Christ in his permanent character as risen from the dead. He was a descendant of David,[a] as my gospel declares. [9]Because I preach this, I am suffering ill-treatment, even to the extent of being imprisoned as if I were a criminal—but the word of God is not chained.

---

[c]Or, that he is able to guard until that Day what I have committed to him. In the only other New Testament occurrences of *parathēkē, deposit* (1 Tim. 6:20; 2 Tim. 1:14), the term clearly denotes the truth which the Lord has entrusted to the ministry and church.

[d]That is, preserve intact, or, keep from distortion.

[e]Possibly this refers to Asiatic acquaintances who were in Rome at the time of Paul's trial but failed to support him (cf. 2 Tim. 4:16), and now had returned to proconsular Asia. Or, Paul may have requested, by letter or by messenger, certain prominent Asians to come to Rome and offer testimony in his behalf but, because of distance or risk to themselves, they did not respond to his appeal.

[a]Cf. 2 Sam. 7:12; Ps. 132:11.

[10]Therefore I endure all these things for the sake of God's chosen ones, in order that they also may obtain the salvation which is in Christ Jesus with eternal glory. [11]Trustworthy is the statement: "If indeed we have died with him, we shall live with him. [12]If we endure, we shall reign with him. If we deny him, he will also deny us. [13]If we prove unfaithful, he remains faithful. For he cannot act contrary to his own nature.[b]

[14]Keep reminding [your listeners of] these things. Charge them before God not to engage in battles about words, for such discussions yield nothing useful but only upset the hearers. [15]Earnestly endeavor to present yourself to God as an approved workman who needs not be ashamed, cutting a straight course by handling properly the word of truth. [16]But avoid all irreverent and empty talk, for those who indulge in it will proceed into more ungodliness, [17]and their doctrine will spread like gangrene. Hymenaeus and Philetus are men like that. [18]They have gone astray from the truth, claiming that the resurrection has already taken place, and they are overthrowing some people's faith. [19]Nevertheless the solid foundation which God established remains standing, bearing this inscription, "The Lord approves[c] those who belong to him,"[d] and "Let everyone who names the Name of the Lord forsake wickedness."[e]

[20]Now in a large house there are not only vessels of gold and silver, but also vessels of wood and clay. Some are for lofty service, and some are for lowly service.[f] [21]Therefore if anyone thoroughly purges himself from those [contaminations to which I have referred], he will be a vessel for honorable service, sanctified, useful to the Master, prepared for any excellent work.

[22]So keep shunning the temptations that are especially alluring to youth, and steadily pursue righteousness, faith, love, peace, in company with people who with pure hearts call upon the Lord. [23]But have nothing to do with foolish, ill-informed speculations, for you know that they cause contentions.

[24]And the Lord's servant must not be contentious but courteous to everyone, skillful in teaching, bearing adverse treatment without resentment. [25]He should correct opponents with meekness, in the hope that God may grant them repentance that leads to full knowl-

[b]Literally, *He is not able to deny himself.*
[c]Cf. Rom. 8:29; Matt. 7:23.   [d]Cf. Num. 16:5.   [e]Cf. Isa. 26:13   [f]Cf. Rom. 9:21.

edge of the truth, [26]and that they may return to their senses [and so escape] from the devil who has held them captive to do his will.[g]

Chapter 3

I want you to know that in the last days difficult times will set in. [2]People in general will be self-centered, money-lovers, boastful, arrogant, abusive, disobedient to parents, ungrateful, without respect for sacred things, [3]without affection for those who should be dear to them because of natural kinship, irreconcilable, slanderers, lacking self-control, brutal, haters of what is good, [4]treacherous, reckless, puffed up with pride,[a] lovers of pleasure rather than lovers of God, [5]maintaining an outward form of godliness but denying its power.

Always turn yourself away from such people. [6]For among them are the sort who sneak into homes and captivate susceptible women[b] who, overwhelmed by their sins and driven by various impulses, [7]are willing to listen to anybody's fancies, but are never able to come into clear knowledge of the truth. [8]Just as Jannes and Jambres[c] opposed Moses, so these [captious] men also set themselves against the truth. They are corrupt in their thinking, and have not stood the test required by the faith. [9]However, they will proceed no further, for their senselessness will become clearly evident to everyone as did that of Jannes and Jambres.

[10]But you have closely followed my teaching, my conduct, my purpose, my faith, my longsuffering, my love, my endurance, [11]the persecutions and sufferings like those which I experienced at [Pisidian] Antioch,[d] at Iconium, [e] [and] at Lystra.[f] You know the kind of persecutions I underwent, and how the Lord delivered me out of them all! [12]In fact, everyone who is determined to live godly in Christ Jesus will be persecuted. [13]Wicked men and impostors will continue to degenerate from bad to worse, deceiving others and being themselves deceived.

---

[g]Literally, *to do the will of that one.* The latter part of the verse could be rendered, and so escape from the devil's captivity to do his [God's] will.

[a]Literally, *be-smoked.* Cf. 1 Tim. 3:6.

[b]Literally, *little women.* The diminutive form, *gunaikaria,* is used in this context as an expression of contempt.

[c]Cf. Exod. 7:10-12, 22.   [d]Cf. Acts 13:14ff.   [e]Cf. Acts 14:1ff.   [f]Cf. Acts 14:6ff.

[14]But as for you, hold fast to the things you have learned and of which you have been assured, because you know [the reliable character of] your teachers. [15]Do not forget that from earliest childhood you have been acquainted with the sacred writings which are able to give you the wisdom which leads to salvation through faith in Christ Jesus. [16]All Scripture is God-breathed and is profitable for teaching, for reproof, for correction, for training in righteousness, [17]so that the man of God may be competent, fully equipped for every excellent work.

Chapter 4

I solemnly charge you in the sight of God and of Christ Jesus, who is to judge the living and the dead, and [I charge you in view of] his appearing and his kingdom: [2]Proclaim the word; stick to your task whether the conditions appear suitable or unsuitable. Reprove, admonish, exhort with the utmost longsuffering and careful instruction. [3]For a time is coming when people will not put up with sound teaching but, in accord with their own cravings, they will secure teachers to tickle their ears. [4]They will deliberately refuse to listen to the truth, but will turn themselves aside to myths. [5]But as for you, keep alert under all circumstances. Endure hardship. Let your work be characterized by evangelism. Perform fully all the duties of your ministry.

[6]For I am already being poured out as a libation,[a] and the time for my departure has arrived. [7]I have fought the good fight. I have finished the race. I have kept the faith. [8]Now there awaits me the victor's crown which the Lord, the righteous Judge, will give to me on that Day—and not to me only, but also to all those who have loved and are longing for his appearing.

[9]Do your best to come to me without delay. [10]Demas, because of his love for the present age, has forsaken me, and has gone to Thes-

---

[a]Or, as a drink offering. The libation, or pouring out of liquids, especially wine, accompanied many Old Testament sacrifices (cf. Exod. 29:40f.; Lev. 23:13, 18, 37; Num. 15:4-10, 24; 28:7-10). Paul's entire ministry had been an offering to God (Rom. 12:1; 15:16). Now has begun the process which will shed Paul's blood. He applies the metaphor of a libation to his approaching martyrdom which will be the last solemn act of his apostolic career.

salonica. Crescens went to Galatia, Titus to Dalmatia. [11]Only Luke is with me. Pick up Mark and bring him with you, for he is useful to me in [God's] service. [12]I am sending Tychicus to Ephesus. [13]When you come, bring the heavy cloak which I left with Carpus at Troas. Bring also the books, especially the parchments. [14]Alexander the metalworker displayed many instances of hostility toward me. The Lord will pay him back according to his deeds. [15]You too must beware of him, for he vehemently opposed our statements.

[16]At the first inquiry into my case,[b] no one came forward to support me but all men forsook me—may it not be held against them! [17]Nevertheless the Lord stood by me and gave me strength, so that through me the gospel might be proclaimed and be heard by all the Gentiles. So I was delivered from the lion's mouth.[c] [18]The Lord will deliver me from every wicked work and bring me safe into his heavenly kingdom. To him be the glory for ever and ever. Amen.

[19]Greet Prisca and Aquila, and the household of Onesiphorus. [20]Erastus remained in Corinth, and I left Trophimus ill at Miletus. [21]Do your best to get here before winter. Eubulus sends greetings to you, as do Pudens and Linus and Claudia and all the brothers.

[22]The Lord be with your[d] spirit. Grace be with all of you.[e]

---

[b]At my first defense.   [c]Cf. Ps. 22:21.
[d]The Greek singular pronoun refers to Timothy.
[e]The Greek plural pronoun includes Timothy and all the fellow Christians who hear or read the letter.

TITUS

Chapter 1

Paul, a servant of God and an apostle of Jesus Christ, for the advancement of the faith of God's chosen ones and of the full knowledge of the truth that promotes godliness, 2based upon the hope of eternal life which God, who is incapable of falsehood, promised long ages ago 3and at the proper time *a* has made known through his word which I, by the command of God our Savior, have been commissioned to proclaim—4to Titus, my genuine son in the faith we hold in common. May gracious favor be yours, and peace, from God the Father and from Christ Jesus our Savior.

5The reason I left you in Crete was that you might correct any deficiencies that still need attention, and appoint elders in each city as I directed you: 6If a man is beyond reproach, the husband of only one wife, and if his children are believers and are not accused of dissipation or insubordination. 7For, as a steward of God, it is necessary that the congregational overseer*b* be a man of irreproachable character, not self-pleasing, not hot-tempered, not addicted to wine,*c* not overbearing, not motivated by a desire for personal gain. 8He must be hospitable, a lover of the good, balanced in judgment, upright, holy, self-controlled, 9holding firmly to the dependable message as it has been taught, so that he may be able both to encourage [believers] and to convince opponents.

10There are many unruly people, foolish talkers, and deceivers, especially those of the circumcision party. 11They must be silenced, because they are subverting entire families by teaching things that are false, [but they do so] for the sake of shameful gain. 12An inhabitant of Crete,*d* one of their own prophets, said, "Cretans are always liars, wicked brutes, idle gluttons." 13That characterization is true. Therefore reprove them sharply, so that they may be sound in the faith,

---

*a*Literally, *in his own times.*   *b*Cf. 1 Tim. 3:2.   *c*Cf. 1 Tim. 3:3.
*d*Literally, *a certain one of them.*

[14]instead of giving their attention to Jewish myths and rules devised by men who turn their backs on the truth. [15]To the pure everything is pure. But to the impure and unbelieving nothing is pure, for they are defiled both in mind and conscience. [16]They profess to know God, but by their deeds they deny him. They are loathsome and disobedient and unfit for any good work.

Chapter 2

But you yourself must speak consistently the things that are in keeping with sound doctrine. [2]Instruct the older men to be clearheaded, worthy of respect, balanced in judgment, sound in faith, in love, in endurance. [3]Similarly the older women must be reverent in their behavior, neither slanderers nor slaves to drink. They should be teachers of what is excellent, [4]in order that they may train the young women to be affectionate toward their husbands and children, [5]balanced in judgment, chaste, efficient in home duties, kind, submissive to their own husbands, so that no damaging reports may be circulated about God's message.

[6]Likewise urge the younger men to be well-balanced in judgment. [7]Make your own life a pattern of commendable conduct, by sincerity in your teaching,[a] by character that commands respect, [8]and by wholesome speech that cannot be condemned. And so the opponent, finding nothing bad to say about us, will be embarrassed into silence.

[9]Exhort slaves to be submissive to their own masters in every respect, to please them well, not to talk back, [10]and not to engage in theft but to show complete trustworthiness, so that in all things they may make attractive the doctrine of God our Savior.

[11]For the grace of God has appeared for the salvation of all mankind, [12]instructing us that, having completely renounced ungodliness and worldly impulses, we should live sensibly and righteously and godly in this present world, [13]eagerly awaiting the blessed hope, even the appearance of the glory of our great God and Savior, Christ Jesus, [14]who gave himself for us, to deliver us from all lawlessness and to purify for his own possession a people eager to do good works. [15]Keep declaring these truths, and exhort and reprove with full au-

---

[a]Or, by purity of doctrine.

thority. Conduct yourself in such a way that no one can slight you or disregard the message.

Chapter 3

Remind your listeners to keep themselves in subjection to the ruling authorities, to be law-abiding, and prepared for any helpful activity, 2to speak evil of no one, to avoid contention, to be considerate of others, showing an attitude of meekness to all men. 3We ourselves were at one time lacking in understanding, disobedient, under deception, enslaved by various cravings and pleasures, wasting our lives in malice and envy, detestable, and hating one another.

4But when the kindness of God our Savior, and his love for man, were manifested, 5not because of any righteous works of our own, but entirely on the basis of his mercy, he saved us by means of the washing of regeneration and the renewing wrought by the Holy Spirit, 6whom he poured forth upon us richly through Jesus Christ our Savior, 7in order that, having been declared righteous by his grace,*a* we might become heirs in the hope of eternal life.

8What I have been saying is trustworthy,*b* and I want you to insist on these essentials so that those who have placed their trust in God may be diligent in the practice of good works. These instructions are good, and will be profitable for the people. 9But avoid foolish speculations and genealogies and dissensions and controversies about the Law, for they are unprofitable and futile. 10After you have given a factious man a first and a second warning, avoid him. 11You may be certain that such an individual is in a perverted condition. He is sinning against knowledge,*c* and he is self-condemned.

12When I send Artemas or Tychicus to [take over your responsibilities in Crete*d*], meet me as soon as you can at Nicopolis, for I have decided to spend the winter there. 13Help Zenas the lawyer and Apollos forward on their travels, and make sure that they lack nothing. 14Our people should learn to keep busy with good works because of such urgent necessities,*e* so that their lives may not be unfruitful.

15All who are with me send their greetings to you. Greet those who love us in the faith. May God's gracious favor be with you all.

---

*a*Literally, *by the grace of that One.*
*b*Or, It is a true saying.   *c*Implied by v. 10.
*d*Literally, *to you.*   *e*Or, to supply the compelling needs.

PHILEMON

Paul, a prisoner for Christ Jesus, and Timothy our brother, to Philemon our beloved friend and fellow worker, ²and to Apphia our sister [in the faith], and to Archippus our fellow soldier, and to the church that meets in your*a* house. ³Grace be to you all, and peace from God our Father and the Lord Jesus Christ.

⁴I give thanks to my God every time I make mention of you in my prayers, Philemon,*b* ⁵because I keep hearing of your devotion and faithfulness toward the Lord Jesus, and [of your concern] for all the saints. ⁶I pray that the liberality which issues from your faith may become even more effective through a deeper realization of the potentialities we have for Christ's service. ⁷Indeed, I had much joy and encouragement [when I first heard] about your expressions of good-will,*c* because through you, my brother, the hearts*d* of the saints have been refreshed.

⁸Although in Christ I have a perfect right to command you to do what is proper, ⁹yet I prefer to appeal to you on the basis of love*c* —being such as I am, Paul, a veteran preacher and now also a prisoner for Christ Jesus. ¹⁰I appeal to you on behalf of a spiritual son of mine. He was converted through my efforts during this imprisonment—I am referring to Onesimus! ¹¹At one time he was useless to you, but now he is useful both to you and to me.

¹²I am sending him back to you, and in so doing it is like sending my own heart. ¹³I would have liked to retain him as a personal helper, so that in your stead he could minister to me during my imprisonment [which I endure] for the sake of the gospel. ¹⁴However, I was not willing to do so without your consent, that your act of kindness might not be compulsory but a matter of your own choice.

¹⁵Perhaps he was separated from you for a time, in order that you might have him back permanently, ¹⁶no longer as a slave, but

*a*The Greek pronoun is singular.   *b*Indicated by singular pronoun.
*c*Greek, *agapē*.   *d*Greek, *splagchna, deep affections.*

159

in a higher relationship—as a beloved brother, especially dear to me but even more to you, both as a man and [as a fellow believer] in the Lord. [17]So if you consider me as your partner [in the faith], receive him as you would receive me. [18]And whatever loss you sustained as a result of what he did, or if he still owes you anything, charge it to my account.

[19]I, Paul, am writing this with my own hand: I myself will pay you in full. (I need not mention your debt. You actually owe me far more than this, because you are under the obligation that outweighs all others—you owe your very self to me.)[e] [20]So, my brother, let me enjoy some repayment from you in the Lord. [By means of this personal favor], satisfy my deep longings for the sake of Christ.

[21]I am writing with complete confidence in your willingness [to comply with my request]. In fact, I am certain that you will do even more than I ask. [22]Just one thing further: Prepare a lodging-place for me; because I hope that, in answer to the prayers of your group, I shall be granted the privilege of visiting you.

[23]Epaphras, who is here in prison with me in [connection with the cause of] Christ Jesus, sends greetings to you, Philemon.[f] [24]So do Mark, Aristarchus, Demas, and Luke, my fellow workers.

[25]May the gracious favor of the Lord Jesus Christ be with the spirit of each of you.

---

[e]Paul was involved, either directly or indirectly, in Philemon's conversion to Christ as a result of the evangelistic thrust into Asia Minor, in which the Phrygian city of Colossae, the home of Philemon, was located (cf. Acts 19:10, 26; Col. 1:7).

[f]Implied by *se*, singular pronoun.